"It is essential for all believers [to understand angels] to partner with them to move into the greatest explosion of miracles and soul harvest in history. This is your how-to book."

Sid Roth, host, *It's Supernatural!*

"Ed Rocha is an amazing minister, pastor, healing evangelist and church planter. I have known him for over a decade, during which time he served as my translator in Brazil. He is a student of the ways of God. He is sensitive to the Holy Spirit and receives revelation from God, which creates in him a strong faith for healing. I love what God is doing in his life, and in his church in Rio de Janeiro, Pier49. I am proud to have Ed as one of my spiritual sons, and proud to have a spiritual son who is an author. He is a great storyteller, making the experiences he shares come to life for the reader. I recommend *Angels—God's Supernatural Agents*."

Dr. Randy Clark, overseer, Apostolic Network of Global Awakening

"Ed brings to us a much-needed understanding of angels and God's purpose in sending them to us. Angelic activity is part of the supernatural realm we are to operate in. Our understanding of this realm and how angels are sent to us by God is vital to bring the Kingdom of God on earth as it is in heaven."

Cal Pierce, international director, Healing Rooms Ministries

"As one who was fished out of a flooding river at age three by an angel, I was already warming up to Ed Rocha's new book. *Angels—God's Supernatural Agents* is not simply a topic of systematic theology, but an encouraging faith-builder, almost on the level of an angelic visitation itself. Just as spiritual gifts are part of God's New Covenant (see Acts 2:39, citing Isaiah 59:21), so angels are part of God's loving covenant with us to protect, feed, inform, warn, rescue and heal. Like the charismata, angels are to be sought as servants from God for our provision. This book engagingly explains and encourages angelic ministry in all its marvelous diversity. This is a great gift for friends who think the only angel they will ever encounter is atop their Christmas tree."

Jon Ruthven, Ph.D., professor emeritus, Regent University; D.Min. mentor, United Theological Seminary; author, *On the Cessation of the Charismata, What's Wrong with Protestant Theology?* and more

ANGELS—
GOD'S SUPERNATURAL
AGENTS

ANGELS—
GOD'S SUPERNATURAL AGENTS

Biblical Insights and True Stories
of Angelic Encounters

ED ROCHA

Chosen
a division of Baker Publishing Group
Minneapolis, Minnesota

© 2017 by Ed Rocha

Published by Chosen Books
11400 Hampshire Avenue South
Bloomington, Minnesota 55438
www.chosenbooks.com

Chosen Books is a division of
Baker Publishing Group, Grand Rapids, Michigan

Printed in the United States of America

Library of Congress Cataloging-in-Publication Data
Names: Rocha, Ed, author.
Title: Angels—God's supernatural agents : biblical insights and true stories of angelic encounters / Ed Rocha.
Description: Minneapolis, Minnesota : Chosen, 2017. | Includes bibliographical references.
Identifiers: LCCN 2016036263 | ISBN 9780800798154 (trade paper : alk. paper)
Subjects: LCSH: Angels—Christianity.
Classification: LCC BT966.3 .R635 2017 | DDC 235/.3—dc23
LC record available at https://lccn.loc.gov/2016036263

17 18 19 20 21 22 23   7 6 5 4 3 2 1

To my wife, Dani—thank you for being
my best friend. I love you.

Contents

Foreword

Any book on the subject of angels stimulates curiosity and, in some cases, warnings. There are good reasons for both responses, which depend largely on a person's background and experience. But angels are real. Very real. Author Ed Rocha does a great job bringing us up to date on the purpose and function of these servants of God.

Not that what is happening in the stories in this book is new. It is not. Stories like these have been happening throughout Church history. It is just that oftentimes supernatural stories get swept under the carpet for fear of confusing people or distracting them from God Himself.

Yet I know of no encounter with the angelic realm that did not result in the increased worship of God. This truth is clearly illustrated by Mary, who bore the Christ child. She responded to her angelic encounter with a profound song of worship. And the shepherds whom the angels visited to announce the birth of Jesus also worshiped.

But some of the old books of revival have had these kinds of reports and experiences edited out of the reprinted versions.

Thankfully Ed does not water down reports of angelic encounters and experiences. In fact, the stories alone are reason enough to buy the book. The insights are brilliant. The biblical basis is enlightening. And the stories—*wow*!

To worship angels is foolish. Equally foolish is to ignore them. God sends them for a purpose, which is to assist us as we "inherit salvation" (Hebrews 1:14). The role of this book is to show us it is legal—and should I say *necessary*—for us to hunger for God's interventions through angels. An unhealthy lack of appetite makes us think we can do life quite well without the assistance of God's assistants. This great paragraph from the book helps us see the need for us to hunger for more:

> There is one factor, however, that does distinguish those who have an encounter with God versus those who do not: *hunger*. God said that those who seek shall find. I believe the opposite is also true. If you are not seeking God's supernatural signs, they will not manifest in your life and ministry. Further, you probably will not recognize signs as coming from God when you see them happening in other people's lives and ministries.
>
> I am convinced that hunger for more of God is the sorting factor between those who experience supernatural encounters and manifestations and those who do not.

Ed also comments that our Western rationalism can keep us out of the realm of the supernatural because we often discount what we cannot see or explain. Our logic and the way we reason, he notes, change once we experience the supernatural.

I have heard people say they do not need angels because they have the Holy Spirit. That sounds so spiritual. But it is foolish. Jesus also had the Holy Spirit—without measure. But the Father sent angels on several occasions to assist and minister to Him. They came in His darkest and most troubling moments. It is not that the Holy Spirit could not do what the angels were sent to do. Jesus limited Himself to live as a man dependent on the Father. As such, He became the model of what we were to become—people living on the edge of two distinct realities, the natural and the supernatural. The Father makes everything for a purpose. And He created and designed angels to assist us in our connection with the unseen world. In fact, every supernatural experience or encounter is to help us anchor our affections in a world we cannot see—a position of balance for the believer who is a citizen of both heaven and earth.

As you read this book, prepare to journey through the Bible to see some of the most significant angelic encounters recorded in Scripture. On top of that, you will read the author's own stories, as well as the credible testimonies of others who have had real encounters with angels. Ed then joins these stories with spiritual principles and Scripture to help us see the biblical basis for this study.

God will use this book, I believe, to increase our faith for more in our own lives and to increase our understanding of what angels are like, what they do, and how they serve God and humans. Read it with anticipation, as I believe it will ignite your heart to hunger for more.

God never turns away those who are truly hungry for more of Him.

Bill Johnson, senior leader, Bethel Church,
Redding, California; author, *God Is Good*
and *The Essential Guide to Healing*
(with Randy Clark)

Acknowledgments

I want to give special thanks to Jane Campbell and Trish Konieczny of Chosen Books. What an awesome team you guys make.

I also want to thank my spiritual family, Pier49 Movement. Your hunger for the supernatural encourages me to pursue more. I love you guys.

1

Angelic Encounters

Are not all angels ministering spirits sent to serve
those who will inherit salvation?

Hebrews 1:14

What are angels? Why were they created? As we see in the Scripture above, angels are ministering spirits. God brought the angels into being before He created the earth, our sun and the firmament. After Creation, He entrusted them with the lives of His children. The angels' primary assignment is to keep us, guard us and minister to us. That is what God created them to do.

The Greek word used for *ministering* in the original text of Hebrews 1:14 is *leitourgikos*, and it comes from the root word *leitourgeō*, which means "to render public service to the state."[1] In the case of the angels, their state is the Kingdom, so the angels are meant to render public service to the Kingdom of God.

Think about this: If the state is the Kingdom, then who are its citizens? Who makes up the Kingdom of God? It is made up of God's people, or in other words, you and me. That's right—the angels are meant to serve us, and I am convinced that they do so to a much greater extent than we are aware of.

17

Who Angels Are Not

Before we go any further on the subject of who the angels are and what they do, let me tell you who the angels are not and what they were not created to do. God did not create the angels as His companions whose primary tasks are to serve and worship Him. Certainly, angels come before the presence of the Lord, and they do serve and worship Him, but I don't believe He created them primarily with those things in mind.

Let me tell you why. When it comes to companionship, some people believe God created the angels because He was lonely and wanted company. We know that cannot be the case. God is a triune being—the Father, the Son and the Holy Spirit. These three have always preexisted as God and have never been lonely.

As far as service, some people believe God created the angels to serve Him. I don't think that can be true either. God is omnipotent. He does not require service, nor does He need any creature to do anything for Him. If He wants something done, it is as good as done already.

When it comes to worship, many people believe God created the angels to worship Him. Even though this is a popular belief, it cannot be true either. God does not suffer from narcissism; He does not need to be worshiped. Worship is not a requirement for Him, and it can never be the primary job description of a created being. The moment worship becomes a duty—the moment it is no longer voluntary—it is no longer true worship. Having to worship as part of your job description makes your act of worship empty of value and void. The angels were not created primarily to worship God, although they do worship Him because their hearts are filled with love and gratitude for who He is.

If God did not create the angels because He was lonely or because He needed servants or because He wanted to be worshiped, then why did He create them? The Bible is very clear when it says that God created them to minister to us, as we saw in Hebrews 1:14 at the start. To understand the truth of that more fully, first we need to understand the timing of their creation. When did He create the angels? Let's have a look at what the Bible says, starting with Exodus 20:11: "For in six days the LORD made the heavens and the earth, the sea, *and all that is in them*, but he rested on the seventh day. Therefore the LORD blessed the Sabbath day and made it holy" (emphasis added). In this verse Moses makes it clear that all God's work on the heavens and earth was done within the six days of Creation. It is important to notice that by "all that is in them" Moses meant all that is in the heavens, so it makes sense to conclude that God created *all that lives* in the heavens within those six days. Keep that idea in mind for a moment.

The word Moses used for *heavens* in this text is the Hebrew word that is transliterated *shamayim*.[2] To know for sure that Moses is not only talking about a physical heaven (the skies), but about even more than that, it is important to know that *shamayim* is also used by the psalmist in Psalm 115:3 in this way: "Our God is in heaven [*shamayim*]." If God lives in *shamayim*, then it cannot only mean skies; it is also the supernatural realm where God chooses to live. I say "chooses to live" because we know that God is not contained by heaven or by any other place. Being omnipresent, He merely chooses to manifest His holy presence in heaven, as well as on earth, as He pleases. Space and time cannot contain Him: "The heavens, even the highest heaven, cannot contain you" (1 Kings 8:27).

A great many Scriptures show us that the angels also dwell in heaven, but we will use only two to establish this point. Genesis 28:12 says that Jacob "had a dream in which he saw a stairway resting on the earth, with its top reaching to heaven [*shamayim*], and *the angels of God* were ascending and descending on it" (emphasis added). Matthew 24:36 says, "But about that day or hour

19

no one knows, not even the angels in heaven, nor the Son, but only the Father." Clearly, the angels reside in *shamayim*, or heaven.

Now look at what the book of Job says:

> Then the LORD spoke to Job out of the storm. He said . . .
>
> "Where were you when I laid the earth's foundation? Tell me, if you understand. Who marked off its dimensions? Surely you know! Who stretched a measuring line across it? On what were its footings set, or who laid its cornerstone—while the morning stars sang together *and all the angels shouted for joy*?"
>
> Job 38:1, 4–7, emphasis added

Remember that I told you to keep something in mind? It was the idea that, based on Exodus 20:11, God created *all that lives in the heavens* within the six days of Creation. Let's recap what we have concluded so far:

1. God created the heavens and the earth on the first day of Creation (see Genesis 1:1).
2. The angels live in the heavens (see Genesis 28:12; Matthew 24:36).
3. All that lives in the heavens was created within the six days of Creation, including the angels (see Exodus 20:11).
4. The angels were already present when God created the earth (see Job 38:1–7).

We put 2 and 2 together and what do we get? That's right— the angels were created on the first day of Creation. Let me break it down for you: If the angels were created within the six days of Creation, and if they were present when God created the earth on the first day, then the angels were created on the first day, when God created the heavens (*shamayim*).

If we agree—as I hope I have established—that God created the angels on the first day of Creation, it helps us understand

20

the answers to our original questions: Who are the angels? What were they created for? As we saw in Hebrews 1:14, *angels are ministering spirits who were created primarily to minister to God's children.* Their primary tasks are to keep us, to guard us and to serve us. I can only conclude that God created the angels on the first day of Creation, before He made His children, so that the angels could serve and minister to them. That makes sense to me. As a good Father, before the arrival of the babies, God made sure He had some nannies in the house, ready to take care of and tend to His beloved children.

Heavenly Messengers

As part of their service to us, God sends His angels as messengers to mankind to fulfill His purposes. The Bible proves this concept all over. We see angels showing people where to go or what to say, guiding them to find water or bringing them food. After Jesus was tempted in the desert, the angels came and served Him. God's angels will always come to serve those who are serving Him. Seek the Lord with all your heart, knowing that He will provide all the resources you need to fulfill His will in your life, whether human or angelical resources.

Angels come from the heavenly realm, where God resides. Of course, we know that God is omnipresent. He is everywhere and anywhere, all the time, and no one can hide from Him (see Psalm 139:7–12). And we know that God can manifest His presence in both a physical and a spiritual manner (see Genesis 1:2; 12:7; 18:1–2; Exodus 3:1–5; 1 Kings 19:1–13). But the Bible also says that He has established His throne in the heavens (see Isaiah 66:1; Matthew 5:34).

A throne is a special seat reserved for a monarch. When the Bible uses the term *throne*, it does so to emphasize God's glory and dignity, and the royal nature of His sovereign rule and existence. I am more and more convinced that the Bible is talking about a real throne of God—a physical throne in the heavenly sphere of reality, of course, but a real throne nonetheless. He does not need such a throne for His sake, because He is transcendent and omnipresent; it is for our sake and for that of the angels. We are not transcendent or omnipresent, and neither are the angels, so it makes sense that God would make Himself available in one spot at a certain time—in this case on His throne in heaven—so that all of us can come before Him in worship and adoration.

Angels come from God. As we have established before, He created them to tend to God's children. One of the primary ways the angels do that is by being messengers of God to mankind.

Angels are spirits whom God created to fulfill His divine purposes and minister in the lives of His children. This is how God intended it to be and how it still is today. There would have been terrible implications throughout human history if God had not sent angels to intervene in key moments and situations. God has chosen to use His angels to interact with us, speak to us, minister to us and help us accomplish the fullness of our calling and destiny.

A number of Scriptures talk about the origin of the angels. Psalm 33:6 (NASB) says, "By the word of the LORD the heavens were made, and by the breath of His mouth all their host." Psalm 148 says, "Praise Him, all His angels; Praise Him, all His hosts! . . . Let them praise the name of the LORD, for He commanded and they were created" (verses 2, 5 NASB).[3]

The English word *angel* comes from the Greek word *ángelos*, which means "messenger."[4] In Hebrew the word for *angel* is *măl'âk*, meaning "to despatch as a deputy; a messenger; specifically, of God."[5] These words are mostly used to describe the angels, the array of spiritual beings God created before He created humans. Angels are essentially God's messengers. They come to communicate God's will to men. They delivered the law to Moses (see Acts 7:52–53) and communicated most of the revelations contained in the books of Daniel, Zechariah and Revelation.

One source says that there are 273 references to angelic visitations in the Bible, 108 times in the Old Testament and 165 times in the New Testament.[6] The exact number of passages that refer to angels can vary, however, depending on what Bible version you use. For example, in the King James Version the word *angel* occurs 201 times in the singular and *angels* occurs 94 times in the plural, for a total of 295 occurrences. In the New International Version those numbers change to 207 times in the singular and 97 times in the plural, for a total of 304 occurrences.[7]

Even though many disregard the subject of angels today, the truth is that they are and always have been very present in our lives throughout the ages. There is no need for us to remain ignorant about the angelic, especially with all the information available in Scripture about these special spirits.

Angels All Over

Angels are all over the Bible. Angels visited Mary and the shepherds to announce the birth of Jesus. An angel visited Zechariah and announced the birth of John the Baptist. An angel appeared to Joseph in a dream to warn him about Herod's plot to kill baby Jesus. Angels served Jesus after the devil tempted Him in the desert. Angels are everywhere in Scripture. Nevertheless, despite all the evidence of angelic manifestations and interactions with people throughout Scripture, we still encounter a lot of resistance when we share stories about angelic encounters today. I wonder why. With so much biblical evidence of angelic interactions, Christians should have no trouble believing stories about angelic visitations and encounters. It is time for us to stop being surprised, shocked or uncertain about stories of present-day angelic encounters.

All over Scripture we see God using angels to minister to His chosen people. They bring healing to the sick, set the captives free and reveal His divine will. God is the same yesterday, today and forever, and if God sent angels in the past, then why would He not send them today? Why is it that we believe in the angels appearing and speaking to people in the Bible, yet it is so hard for us to believe it now when someone says, "An angel came to me and said . . ."?

I think it is about time that the Church opens its eyes to see and its arms to embrace the reality of angels. All over the world angelic manifestations have increased, even among unbelievers. Sometimes these encounters lead them to Christ. Sometimes such an encounter delivers someone from certain death, which is also, in the case of an unbeliever, a deliverance from hell.

Yes, God still sends His angels to interact with us and intervene in our history, and that is what this book is all about. If you are still with me at this point, chances are that you really like the subject of the angelic and you want to learn more about it. If that is the case, then you have the right book. In the pages that follow, I will take you on an awesome journey through the Bible and show you some of the most significant angelic encounters recorded in Scripture. I will also share with you some exciting and edifying testimonies from the lives of people in our day who have had personal encounters with angels. I will share with you the spiritual principles behind these scriptural passages and present-day encounters and talk about how you can apply those principles to your life today.

Life with God is supposed to be a breathtaking and adventurous ride packed with supernatural encounters. Amazing testimonies of encounters with angels are waiting for you on the next pages, along with a look at some other supernatural manifestations people encounter that are a blessing. I want to invite you to get in on this adventurous journey into the supernatural realms of God. So buckle up, raise your hands up high and enjoy the ride!

2

Healing in Their Wings

Of the angels he says, "Who makes his angels
winds . . ."

Hebrews 1:7 WEB

"Do you want me to tell you what I see?" I asked Randy Clark
as we stood on the stage in front of thousands of people in this
renewed Baptist church in Rio de Janeiro, Brazil. Dr. Randy
Clark, the founder of Global Awakening Ministries, is also my
spiritual father and mentor.

"Yes!" Randy answered me with a smile, as excited as a little
boy in the candy shop.

For a few seconds Randy and I just stood there whispering
to one another, facing the crowd and sensing what God was
doing. At least four thousand spiritually hungry Brazilians were
in the church that night, and the atmosphere was electric with
the presence of God. The anointing was particularly intense.
Many people, even the visiting unbelievers, later reported that
they had felt the intensity of God's presence there.

"I see angels," I told Randy, "dozens and dozens of angels coming in from the left, and they're carrying healing in their wings."

"I feel their presence, but I don't see them," Randy told me, smiling. "What are they doing?"

"They're flapping their wings over the crowd in the back, right over there." I pointed to the left, toward the back of the building. It was a hot and humid summer night, as most of the nights are in Rio.

Randy turned his microphone back on and announced, "There are dozens of angels coming from that side of the building. I don't see them, but Ed does, and it bears witness in my spirit because I had felt that there were angels there before he told me. . . ."

He briefly explained to the church that some people sense the presence of angels, while others have their spiritual eyes opened and are able to see them in the spirit realm.

"Get ready, all of you who are in that area in the back." He tiptoed in excitement as he said it. "The angels are stretching their wings, and they're about to flap them over you. I believe that when they do, God will release a healing anointing over this place."

Those in the crowd raised their hands up high, expecting their blessing.

Randy turned his microphone to mute again and said to me, "Tell me what's happening."

I kept watching as the angels stood with their wings spread apart over the crowd. Suddenly, as if they had just been waiting for Randy to announce it, they started flapping them.

"Now—they've started flapping their wings now," I whispered to Randy.

He waited to see if there would be any confirmation in the natural of what I had just seen, and surely there was. Out of the blue, *inside* this building a wind blew on those people. Many of them started to shake.

Randy turned his microphone back on and announced, "Now—they're flapping their wings right now—receive it! Receive your healing. Receive your touch."

A whole section of hundreds of people started to shake and fall in the Spirit as the angels flapped their wings over them. Later, when we turned on the camera and interviewed some of the people who were healed, we found out that all the sick in that particular section of the church had received their healing.

The Faith of the Centurion

We know God uses His angels to fulfill His purposes. That concept is clearly implicit (please forgive the oxymoron) in Matthew 8:5–13. In this text we see a centurion whose servant needed healing and who believed that Jesus had authority over spiritual forces and beings:

> When Jesus had entered Capernaum, a centurion came to him, asking for help. "Lord," he said, "my servant lies at home paralyzed, suffering terribly."
>
> Jesus said to him, "Shall I come and heal him?"
>
> The centurion replied, "Lord, I do not deserve to have you come under my roof. But just say the word, and my servant will be healed. For I myself am a man under authority, with soldiers under me. I tell this one, 'Go,' and he goes; and that one, 'Come,' and he comes. I say to my servant, 'Do this,' and he does it."
>
> When Jesus heard this, he was amazed and said to those following him, "Truly I tell you, I have not found anyone in Israel with such great faith. I say to you that many will come from the east and the west, and will take their places at the feast with Abraham, Isaac and Jacob in the kingdom of heaven. But the subjects of the kingdom will be thrown outside, into the darkness, where there will be weeping and gnashing of teeth."

> Then Jesus said to the centurion, "Go! Let it be done just as you believed it would." And his servant was healed at that moment.

> Matthew 8:5–13

This centurion believed that Jesus could send these forces out to accomplish His will and to heal. The centurion even draws a parallel between his own authority in sending soldiers back and forth under his command and what Jesus could do. It is also interesting to note that just like any human army, the angelic realm includes different ranks. For example, there are the cherubim, the seraphim and the archangels. (I talk about the angelic hierarchy in more detail in chapter 12.)

Jesus did not correct the centurion's remarks. Rather, He praised him for his faith, meaning that his concept was right on. In other words, the angels of the Lord indeed are under His command. We see all over Scripture that God sends them to bring about His sovereign will. In some cases such as the centurion's servant, that includes healing. I know without a shadow of doubt that on the night when I had that open vision of angels in the meeting with Randy, God used angels to bring healing to those people, thus confirming the word that was being preached and increasing the people's faith in the name of Jesus.

Angels, by their own power, cannot heal anyone. Likewise, we human beings, by our own power, cannot heal anyone. The power to heal comes from God. The Bible does not give a single account of angels healing anyone by their own power. Nevertheless, I believe the angels are carriers and executors of God's will. I believe He sends His angels with healing to His people. I also believe demons cause many infirmities, and the mere presence of the angelic can drive these afflicting spirits away, along with the infirmities they cause.

I think it was one of the above that happened to the centurion's servant. The centurion, a man under authority himself, well understood how a hierarchy of authority works. He knew that Jesus, being Lord of Hosts, had angels under His authority that He could send to where the sick servant was to bring healing. Jesus praises the centurion for his faith and does not correct his assumption, confirming that God does indeed use His angels for such services.

Jesus also said once, "Do you think I cannot call on my Father, and he will at once put at my disposal more than twelve legions of angels?" (Matthew 26:53 NIV). God sends His angels to serve His children, as Hebrews 1:14 says. When what we need is a healing, that is what an angel will bring. That was the correct assumption of the centurion, confirmed by Jesus. The Lord even clearly told him, "Go! Let it be done just *as you believed it would*" (Matthew 8:13, emphasis added). In other words, I believe Jesus was saying, "Let My holy angels, who were sent by the Father to serve Me, go to that place now with healing for your servant." And the Bible says that the centurion's servant was healed at that very moment.

In the parallel passage in Luke 7:1–10, we find that the centurion's servant was healed at the very moment when Jesus declared his healing. Jesus was amazed that the centurion had such a revelation and demonstrated such faith (see Matthew 8:10; Luke 7:9). Scripture does not say anything about the disciples going to the centurion's, and even if they had gone, they could not have traveled fast enough to witness the healing because the centurion's servant was healed the very moment Jesus declared his healing. Besides, there is no report that anyone was seen praying for the sick man; all it took were Jesus' words. Whom do you think Jesus could have sent? Beings who were invisible, who could travel fast and who could bring divine healing with them? Let's check that list again: (1) invisible, (2) amazingly fast, (3) able to bring healing from God. Sound like an angel to you?

New Body Parts

Recently I was on one of our mission trips, and after a meeting I ended up praying for a gentleman who had lost most of the hearing in both ears and therefore had to use hearing aids. This man came to me and said, "I read your book about healing, and I'm ready to get healed myself."

"Awesome," I replied. "What's your name?" (Which is my very first question when I pray for the sick.[1])

"Tom," he quickly and firmly answered as he removed his hearing aids. "Here," he handed them to me. "I won't be needing these anymore!"

"Oh, look at the souvenirs," I said, smiling as I took them from him.

"What?" he said, placing his hand like a shell behind his ear.

"Nothing!" I shouted. "Never mind!" I placed the hearing aids in his shirt pocket, smiled again and then placed my hand over his ears and prayed. The moment I started praying, a few people gathered around. I saw an angel hastily flying into a warehouse in heaven. He picked up something from a shelf and quickly flew down to where we were.[2] The angel came and stood right beside Tom. He had one of those old-fashioned doctor's head mirrors on his forehead, and he looked intently inside Tom's ear. Then he quickly pulled up some sort of instrument, stuck it inside Tom's ear and started working on it.

The moment the angel placed the instrument in Tom's ear, Tom flinched, bent down, squinted his eyes and let out a little cry: "Ouch!" He stuck his finger into his ear and shook it.

"Tom, it's okay; don't panic. There's an angel tinkering with your ear right now." I told him what I was seeing in the spirit realm.

"I feel something, like there's a worm moving in there or something," Tom said with a wrinkled face.

"That's okay, Tom," I reassured him. "I saw the angel enter a spare parts warehouse in heaven and pick up new parts for your ear, and then dash down here. He's standing by your side right now, replacing the old parts with the new ones he brought with him." I smiled as I continued to pray. At this point most of the team had gathered around and were helping me in prayer and intercession for Tom.

"Father," I prayed out loud, "thank You for sending Your angel with new parts for Tom's ear. We want to partner with him and enter into agreement with Your good and perfect will for Tom. Thank You, Papa God." I continued to pray along those lines, and then I said, "Angel of the Lord, thank you for coming. Thank you for bringing these new parts for Tom's ear. Thank you for what you are doing in his ear, and thank you for your ministry. You go on and do what the Father sent you to do; we bless what you are doing in Tom's ear, in Jesus' name."

The whole thing did not last more than five minutes before Tom started to laugh and shout, "I can hear! I'm healed!" When the team around him started to clap and shout for joy, Tom immediately covered his ears and shouted, "Not too loud, guys! Ouch! Not too loud!"

Everyone cried out and shouted for joy even more as they realized that Tom now could not only hear without the hearing aids, but could hear really well—to the point that their shouting was too loud for his brand-new ears.

"C'mon, 1, 2, 3 . . ." I shouted to the crowd with a big smile, and they replied, "Praise Jesus!"

I ended up praying for more people on the team itself that morning. In the end we had a total of six deaf ears open and another three people who were healed from eye problems, all through the ministry of the angels. Yes, they are ministering spirits sent in our favor.

It is time for you to acknowledge the ministry of the angels and to expect that God will send them to minister to you. Remember that most of the time God acts according to our expectations. Jesus often linked the operation of miracles to people's faith (see Matthew 9:22, 29; Mark 5:34; Luke 17:19). What do you think would have happened in the case of the centurion, or in other cases of healing in Scripture, if no one had had any expectation that a miracle would take place? I will tell you what would have happened—the same thing that happened for the people of Nazareth, who had no faith in Jesus—nothing. He could not perform miracles there because of their lack of faith (see Mark 6:1–6). Angels would not have been dispatched to heal the centurion's servant if the centurion had not had the expectation for it.

If you do not expect an angel to come and bring your miracle, then you will not have one. But if you do have an expectation that God will send an angel with your miracle, He will likely act in accordance with your expectation. He wants to come into agreement with what we believe for. I want to encourage you to believe in the ministry of His angels. More than that, I want you to expect God to send them to minister to you and bring about your miracle. Why not? Why not today? Why not now? All you have to do is believe!

3

"Pleez, Dun Shoo!"

For he will command his angels concerning you to
guard you in all your ways.

Psalm 91:11

I love to sit with the wise and experienced, the gray-haired. I
cherish the counsel of the wise. I enjoy visiting with them and
learning from their wisdom. The following true story is an
eyewitness account I heard on a visit with an old friend who is
a Korean War veteran.

The light of dawn shone brightly through my eyelids. I blinked.
A few snowflakes came dancing with the cold breeze and got
stuck to the mud on my face. As I sat up, this huge throbbing
pain hit me hard on the side of my head. I brought my hand up
and pressed the side where it hurt, which soothed it some, but
the pain wouldn't go away. I brought my hand back down and
felt something peel off my forehead. It was dried blood that had
covered a small cut over a bump. I involuntarily showed my teeth.

I looked for my M1 rifle . . . gone. I tapped my uniform and realized that my load was gone, all of it, including my sidearm and all my ammo. Someone had frisked me clean. All they left behind was my uniform, my boots and my helmet. I knew it was my helmet because I had written "Born Again" on it. In the beginning I heard a lot of jokes about that, but eventually it became my war name. Before I left home for Korea, I had determined in my heart that I would preach the Gospel to my fellow soldiers. One way or another, they would hear the Good News. I wasn't the most popular kid in the battalion, but I kept my promise.

Four bodies were lying on the floor a few feet away from me. I got up and searched them for supplies, ammo, anything I could find. I was late; someone had already cleaned them up, probably the same guy or guys who had stripped me of my gear. I lined up the bodies and took a good look at them—all young boys. I knew most of them by name. I remember, back in the camp, telling them about my faith in the Lord Jesus Christ. Some of them had laughed at me; others had lowered their eyes respectfully. Despite their faith or lack thereof, these young American soldiers had fought and died for their country, and they deserved a Christian burial. I took my shovel and started digging holes deep and long enough for each of them. I don't know how long it took me, but it wasn't long. Still wet from the recently melted snow, the dirt was easy to dig through. I placed the bodies in the holes and covered them with dirt and then rocks. I took the young guys' shoelaces and some twigs and made four crosses, which I stuck at the top of each grave to hang the occupant's dog tags on. These weren't the best graves I'd ever seen—certainly not the graves these soldiers deserved—but I did my best, considering the circumstances.

Finally, I placed my helmet on my chest and sang "Amazing Grace." That was my pastor's favorite song back at my church in Kansas. He sang it every time he did a funeral back home. Before I could finish the song, I heard five pairs of Commie boots marching down my way. The men wearing them had their guns pointed straight at me.

It was only then that I realized how dumb I had been. I should have dragged the bodies back into the woods and buried them there, not out in the open. "Dear Lord Jesus!" was all I managed to say as I felt the bitter taste of adrenaline fill up my throat. I imagined these guys shooting me. I thought of my family back home, and my life raced through my mind. I guess in the end you think of the beginning. At least, that's what I did. I remembered Mom and Dad, Grandma and Sunday school. I remembered some prophetic words I had received in tent revival meetings: *One day you will be an evangelist and win many souls to the Lord.* At that point I already had led my cousin Brent to the Lord and had witnessed to a bunch of people, but I don't remember leading more than two or three others to Christ. And right now, it surely didn't feel as if the prophecies of becoming a great evangelist would come to pass.

I was tired, my hands were shaking and my knees were hurting. The throbbing pain in my head had gotten worse. A cold breeze soothed the pain, however, and I could smell the snow-wet grass. I thought of heaven. Would this be my end?

The Commies were getting closer, and by now I could see their breath as they marched toward me. I raised my eyes to heaven and prayed for protection. I don't remember the exact words, but it was something along the lines of, *Father God, if You still have something to accomplish through my life, I need a miracle. If not, please let them make it quick.*

I couldn't understand what happened next. The five North Korean soldiers halted a few yards away from me, wide-eyed, as if they had seen a ghost. One by one they placed their guns at my feet, took a few steps back and knelt down with their hands behind their heads. In their broken English, they kept saying something that sounded like, "Pleez, dun shoo!"

I was shocked! My heart was racing, my head was throbbing and I thought I would throw up. But in a split second my military training kicked in. With my eyes fixed on those five men, I picked up their carbines and hung them over my neck and left arm. Then I picked up their handguns and stuck them around my belt. I noticed that for some reason the men were barely looking at me. They kept their hands up and stared straight up over my head.

I jerked my head around instinctively, trying to see what they were staring at, but there was nothing there. I didn't understand it, but I had no time to figure it out; all I had in mind was my survival. Besides, I was shaking so hard I could barely think.

I took a few steps away from them and motioned with my rifle, saying, "Go! March!" I nodded and pointed forward.

I don't know if they understood my English or just the gestures, but they got up and walked. I had no idea where we were marching to; I just kept them moving in the open field, where I could keep them in my sight. We didn't march for long before we found what was left of my troop, resting under some trees by a creek. Someone on watch yelled that we were coming. The whole company quickly jumped to their feet, with rifles pointed straight at the surrendering Commies. I marched them single file into camp. A bunch of soldiers came running to help, made them kneel down and roughly handcuffed them.

"Dadgummit, Private Born Again!" Commander Harvey yelled at me as I marched in with the prisoners. "How on earth did you manage to pull that one off?" He was yelling so loudly that he spit out some of the tobacco he was chewing on.

"I don't know, sir," I said as I grabbed a steaming mug of hot coffee somebody brought me. Commander Harvey could see the fear and astonishment in my eyes. I told him how the whole thing took place.

"Private Tyler!" Commander Harvey yelled again. Private Tyler was the only one in our entire regiment who could speak some Korean. Tyler came forward on the double.

"Sir, yes, sir!" Private Tyler pushed up his glasses.

Commander Harvey slowly walked back and forth in front of the handcuffed enemy soldiers, who were kneeling on the frozen North Korean ground. Snow crunching under his boots, he crouched down to better see their faces. His eyes bugged out, and his eyebrows went way up on his forehead.

"Private Tyler," said the commander, "would you please ask them Commies over here why on earth have they surrendered to Private Born Again?"

"Sir, yes, sir!" said Private Tyler, who stepped in front of them and spoke in Korean. They answered him rather emphatically.

"Sir," Private Tyler said, his brows pressed together, "they said they surrendered because they were outnumbered."

"Outnumbered?" shouted Commander Harvey, the skin on his forehead crumpling in a bunch of creases. He turned to me and shouted, "What are they talking about, Private Born Again?"

"Sir, I have no idea, sir," I said.

"Private Tyler, ask them whom they think they were out-numbered by, will you?" he shouted.

Private Tyler did as he was told, and they answered rather emphatically again. He translated their reply: "Sir, they said they surrendered to the tall soldiers in white, sir." Tyler shrugged his shoulders.

"Will you please ask them Commies over here who the heck were these soldiers in white?"

Private Tyler asked the North Koreans and they answered back, sounding a little frustrated this time. Tyler looked down, as if trying to process the information.

"So?" demanded Commander Harvey. "What on God's good earth did they say now, Private Tyler?"

Tyler looked at him as if trying to put his thoughts in order.

"Spill it out, son," yelled the commander, trying not to spit his tobacco out of his mouth again.

"Sir," Tyler finally said, "they said there were twelve soldiers in white, all ten feet tall, heavily armed and . . ." Tyler paused, looking down at the ground.

"And what, Private?" yelled the commander.

Private Tyler took his helmet off and held it over his chest.

"For goodness' sake, Tyler," the commander spat his tobacco and leaned forward, "finish the translation, will ya?"

Shaking, Tyler looked up. "They say the white soldiers are here, sir, all around us right now."

The commander stared at the five handcuffed Commies and suddenly understood why they would not look up. For the longest time ever, we just stood there. Nobody dared move a muscle; nobody made a sound. All you could hear was the morning breeze whistling through the tree branches around us.

Suddenly, that unbelieving commander took off his helmet, held it tightly over his chest, bowed his head and knelt down. One by one, all the other soldiers did the same. Some were quicker than others, but even some of the most hardened hearts put out their cigarettes, spat out their tobacco, placed their helmets over their chests and knelt down as this amazing fear of God fell on us all. Some of us, starting with me, could not hold back our tears.

"Would you pray for us, Born Again?" the commander asked, not daring to look up.

I think that was the first time I ever heard Commander Harvey talk in a normal tone of voice. I felt a rush of energy run all over my body. I didn't know it then, but it was the anointing of the Holy Spirit falling over me. I told my fellow soldiers to repeat the sinner's prayer after me. They did, all committing their lives to Christ. I told Tyler to translate it all to the Commies and explain to them who the tall soldiers were. They also prayed the sinner's prayer, giving their lives to Jesus Christ, the Son of God.

What an amazing testimony. I cannot help but have tears in my eyes every time I think of it. I feel as if it takes me there, and I witness the holy platoon of angels surrounding those Communist soldiers. Isn't it amazing that the Bible promises that God will send His angels to watch over us? They will protect us in times of danger and need: "For the angel of the Lord is a guard; he surrounds and defends all who fear him" (Psalm 34:7 NLT).

Angel Stats

A new Associated Press-GfK poll shows that 77 percent of adults today believe angels are real.[1] People have always associated angels with the Christmas story, but the poll shows that many people see angels as a year-round presence. It also shows that belief in angels is primarily tied to a person's religion, with 88 percent of Christians, 95 percent of evangelical Christians and 94 percent of those who attend a religious service of any kind weekly saying they believe in angels.

According to the poll, the belief in angels is spread among more than the religious. Most non-Christians also think angels exist, as do more than 4 in 10 of those who never attend religious services. These numbers mirror a 2006 AP-AOL poll, which found that 81 percent of the American public believed in angels.

As I prepared to write this book, I started a survey of my own and asked one thousand people (all born-again believers) three simple questions:

1. Have you ever asked God to send His angels in your aid?
2. Do you believe God sent His angels?
3. If you believe He sent them, did you . . .
   a. see them
   b. feel them
   c. neither, but you know they were there

The results of the survey were interesting. The majority of people, 70 percent, answered that they had prayed to God and that He had sent His angels to intervene on their behalf. Out of that majority, 90 percent answered *Yes, God sent His angels to intervene in our situation*; 5 percent answered *I'm not sure;* and 5 percent answered *No, I don't think the angels came at all.*

It is also interesting to note that out of those who answered that God had sent His angels, 10 percent claim that they saw the angels; 60 percent claim that they felt the angels; and 30 percent claim that they neither saw nor felt them—they just somehow knew the angels were there.

Biblically and statistically speaking, angels are a constant part of our lives. God sends them to save us from harm, to make us miss that train that might crash. Or to make us drop a book and slow down just enough to miss that piano about to fall on our head. Or to protect us from demons who surround us like lions, looking for people who are disconnected from God, in whose lives they can steal, kill and destroy (see 1 Peter 5:8; John 10:10).

Angels Come to Serve Us

One thing we learn from Jesus Himself is that we should not petition the Lord our God to send His angels whenever we feel like it. We should not be daredevils hanging from the edge of tall buildings, nor should we presume upon the Lord in any way by doing foolish things while trusting the angels to protect us from harm. No, no, no. That is exactly how the devil tried to tempt Jesus in the desert:

> Then the devil took him into the holy city. He set him on the pinnacle of the temple, and said to him, "If you are the Son of God, throw yourself down, for it is written, 'He will put his angels in charge of you.' and, 'On their hands they will bear you up, so that you don't dash your foot against a stone.'"
>
> Jesus said to him, "Again, it is written, 'You shall not test the Lord, your God.'"
>
> Matthew 4:5–7 web

When we truly and fully submit to the Father, as Jesus did, God will send His angels to us, as He sent them to Jesus:

Then Jesus said to him, "Get behind me, Satan! For it is written, 'You shall worship the Lord your God, and you shall serve him only.'"

Then the devil left him, and behold, *angels came and served him.*

Matthew 4:10–11 WEB, emphasis added

The angels came not because Jesus demanded it or commanded them to do so, but rather, because the Father sent them. The Bible promises that God will order His angels to come down and protect you, serve you and provide for your needs (see Psalm 91:11; Hebrews 1:14). Whatever you are going through, trust God and ask Him to send His holy angels to aid you. He promised He would, and He will.

4

Angelic Intervention

Believers, look up—take courage. The angels are
nearer than you think.

Billy Graham

If you have never seen an angel, it does not mean you cannot
see them. Don't dismiss angelic encounters as something that
you cannot experience. God is the same yesterday, today and
forever (see Hebrews 13:8). The angelic encounters that you see
in the Bible *still happen* today. If you have never experienced
anything like that, but you would like to, ask God to open your
spiritual eyes so you can see His angels.

It is important that you start looking around intently and
being spiritually sensitive to the angels. They are all around.
"Seek and you will find" (Matthew 7:7). I strongly encourage
you to pray and ask the Father to surround you with His glorious
angels. Always be praying for the Father to send His angels to
minister in your favor. You never know when your next visitation will be.

Hundreds of books have been written about angels. Some of the angelic accounts they describe predate the Bible; others are written by modern authors and are fresh off the press. Many of these books are based on personal visions. Ancient Babylonian scrolls, the book of Enoch, the gospel of Judas and other Apocrypha contain angelic stories. But for us as Christian believers, what matters is what the Bible has to say. We believe the Bible is the Word of God; therefore, it is our rule of faith and practice. We must make sure that whatever we believe about angels is well guarded by the boundaries of Scripture, lest we find ourselves drifting away from sound doctrine. We can learn about angels from many passages in the Bible. In all the biblical passages that mention God's holy angels, we see that above all other offices the angels may have, they are His holy messengers. By sending angels to bring us messages, God interacts with people through them. The angels also serve us and minister to our needs.

Helping Wings

The Bible tells us that God will send His angels to answer His children when they cry out for help. The spirit world is real, and angels are real. Your Father in heaven will send them to work on your behalf, if you ask Him. We know this because Jesus Himself gave us a legal precedent for it: "Don't you think that I could call on my Father to send more than twelve legions of angels to help me now?" (Matthew 26:53 GWT).

Whatever your needs are, go ahead and pray. Ask the Father to send His angels to operate on your behalf. I believe He will do it. Consider that God sent an angel to deliver Daniel in the lions' den (see Daniel 6:22). The angel shut the lions' mouths and Daniel suffered no harm. God also sent an angel to help Moses. When Moses was leading the Israelites out of Egypt, the

Lord told him, "I am going to send an angel in front of you, to guard you on the way and to bring you to the place that I have prepared" (Exodus 23:20 NRSV). And I shared this next verse once already, but when we talk about whether or not God sends His angels, I do not think we can get enough of it, so here it is in another translation: "The angel of the LORD encamps around those who fear him, and delivers them" (Psalm 34:7 NRSV).

Elisha had angelic experiences. In 2 Kings 6:17, we see that he and his servant were surrounded by an army of angels God sent to protect them. When Elijah was afraid and running for his life in 1 Kings 19, an angel appeared to provide food and water for his journey.

In the Garden of Gethsemane, Jesus asked the Father to deliver Him from the cup that was to come, and an angel came from heaven to strengthen Him (Luke 22:43). You may say, "Yeah, but He only sent angels to important people like the prophets and Jesus." That is not true. God sent angels to common folks like you and me. We will talk more about that in the next chapter.

God is the same yesterday, today and forever; He does not change. He used angels to help people in the Bible, and if He is the same, that means He still sends angels to help us today. Yes, angels are still among us.

Supernatural Item Recovery

I have heard many stories about angels bringing lost or stolen items back to people. Bill Johnson has a famous sermon called "I Want My Knife Back" in which he shares powerful testimonies of people who have received items back supernaturally. My wife and I have also had supernatural item-recovery experiences, as have other people at our church. I believe these experiences involved angels. In my ministry travels, I love to sit down and talk with people about God over a good cup of coffee or tea. In one of these precious moments, a brother shared a beautiful story of supernatural item recovery that involved angels. I think his story will light up your faith to expect the same thing to happen for you.

A few years ago on a certain rainy night, my wife and I went out for dinner. Despite the rain, we had a great time at the restaurant. When we were ready to leave, I asked for the bill. The waiter brought it to me and laid it on the table with a courteous smile. I pulled out my wallet and paid for the meal. We left the restaurant and ran back to the car, trying to avoid the rain as much as possible. We drove away, and we were almost home when I realized I wasn't feeling the volume of my wallet on my back pocket. I reached for it in my pocket and it wasn't there. Suddenly I realized I must have dropped it. I started praying under my breath, asking the Father to send His angels to find my wallet for me.

My wife noticed I was praying and asked, "What's wrong?"

"Nothing," I said, which is my natural response whenever she asks me that question.

"Something is wrong," she said. "I can tell when you're worried."

"How?" I asked.

"When you're worried, you frown when you pray," she said.

"I lost my wallet," I confessed.

"Then let's go back and look for it," she said.

"Honey, the mall is closed by now, and besides . . ." I shrugged my shoulders, "we're almost home already."

"So what's the plan? What are you gonna do about it?" She shot both questions at me in one breath.

"Well," I said, "I'm asking Father to send an angel back to find my wallet for me."

We had never gone through something like this before, and my wife had an "I can't believe what you just said" kind of look on

45

her face. But at this point in our marriage, we had gone through enough miracles and supernatural experiences that by now we knew that nothing was impossible. She started praying with me.

We got home, and I must confess, I was not calm. My heart was racing. I almost went back after my wallet myself, but I was trying to remain peaceful and stay in faith. As soon as I opened the door of the house, I had a picture in my mind. I saw my wallet inside the top drawer of my bedroom dresser. I ran to the bedroom.

"What are you doing?" my wife asked.

"I know where it is!" I shouted.

"Where?" she shouted back, running after me.

I got into the bedroom, with my wife right beside me. I opened the drawer slowly and there it was, sitting in the middle of the drawer, still wet from the rain. I picked it up and showed it to her. She was dumbfounded.

"But I saw you pick up your wallet and pay the bill at the restaurant." Her words came out muffled through her fingers.

I couldn't stop my nervous laughter. "I know I did, babe," I said. "I paid for dinner with it. I must have dropped it in the parking lot when we ran to the car because of the rain."

I couldn't stop smiling, either; I was so thankful. I held my wife's hand and prayed, "Father, thank You for Your love. Thank You for taking care of us. Thank You for sending Your angel to pick up my wallet, bring it back and put it here in my drawer. Thank You that it is still wet from the rain; this really strengthens our faith. Thank You, Father!"

The Power of the Testimony

Wherever I preach, I share such testimonies. In one church I visit regularly, I had someone share another testimony with me about supernatural item recovery. This young man told me that on a certain Monday evening right after I had spoken at his church, he stopped his car at a red light. Two burglars on a motorcycle pointed a gun at him and took his wallet, his watch and his brand-new cell phone, with all his business contacts in it that he did not have stored anywhere else. I could tell you what happened next, but I would rather share the story with you in his exact words:

I was shaking so much that I couldn't keep driving. I parked my car at a nearby mall and lowered the window all the way down to catch some fresh air. I got out and sat on the curb, upset and crying. It wasn't a prayer; it was more like me thinking to myself: *Why? Why do bad things happen to good people, God?* And that's when I heard your voice, Ed, whispering in my head: *Ask God to send His angels.*

I think I heard that because it was Monday and I had just heard you preach about angels the day before. Anyhow, I looked up into the sky and it was getting dark. I could already see a few stars. For whatever reason, I chose the brightest one and kept my eyes on it. I could smell a fresh breeze that swayed through the branches of some pine trees nearby. I placed my hand over my chest and felt my heart pound. I prayed out loud, "Father, I do not deserve this, but, by Your goodness and mercy, I pray, please send me Your angels. Let them help me recover my cell phone and, if possible, my watch and wallet, too. In Jesus' name I pray, Amen."

Barely had the words come out of my mouth when I saw this—the best way I can describe it is as if a man dressed in pure lightning ran at high speed by my car and tossed something inside. Startled, I got up. Before I could think of anything else, I looked inside the car to see what he had tossed in. To my surprise, it was my cell phone, my watch and my wallet!

I looked around to see if I could find the man dressed in lightning, but he was gone. I have goose bumps all over my body just remembering that experience. I got in my car, and with tears running down my cheeks I thanked God for hearing my prayer and sending His holy angels to help me.

I want to encourage you to live in this level of faith and ask the Father for supernatural item recoveries. Whenever you lose something or, God forbid, have something stolen from you, pray with faith and ask the Father to send His angels to find and retrieve the item for you. Keep trusting, keep calm and keep praying. Don't let fear or doubt find a place in your heart. If they try to come in (and most of the time they will), rebuke them. Turn your mind and your thoughts toward the goodness of our Father in heaven and ask Him to send His angels. Then fill your mind with thanksgiving and worship.

Angel Caught on Tape

Remember that our Father will send His angels to help us and serve us, according to His will. Can such angelic intervention be caught on camera? Many people would say yes. Many believe that they have recorded angels with their video cameras or phones.

I have seen such images. In fact, I have one, and I will tell you more about that in chapter 9 on seeing angels. But I also want to share with you an interesting video of an angel caught by a shopping mall's security camera. You can look it up online at https://vimeo.com/147844409. In it, you will clearly see this angel coming from above, over the parking lot. He picks up something from the ground and takes off at lightning speed.

I wonder if this angel was sent to find and retrieve someone's lost wallet or some other valuable item. If you believe in angels, as I do, watching this video definitely will increase your faith. Begin to pray and ask the Father to send His angels to minister to you, and then watch what happens.

5

Entertaining Angels

Do not neglect to show hospitality to strangers,
for by this some have entertained angels without
knowing it.

Hebrews 13:2 NASB

One of the reasons God sends His angels to interact with us
is that He hears us when we cry out for help. His angels come
when we pray. I think it is fascinating how God sends His angels
to watch over us, even over the infants and children among us.
Look what happened with Ishmael, the young son of Abraham
and Hagar: "The angel of God called to Hagar out of the sky,
and said to her, 'What ails you, Hagar? Don't be afraid. For God
has heard the voice of the boy where he is'" (Genesis 21:17 WEB).

In this passage we see that God heard Ishmael crying in the
desert, and He sent His angel to aid the youth and his mother.
Ishmael was not even crying out to God, but God heard his cry
and intervened for his good by sending an angel to help.

Of course, we know that this was not just any young man; he was special because he was a son of Abraham. God had a covenant with his father and had given a promise to Abraham: "On that day the LORD made a covenant with Abram and said, 'To your descendants I give this land'" (Genesis 15:18). In order for His Word not to fall to the ground (see 1 Samuel 3:19), God made sure an angel would be guarding that boy. God always fulfills His promises. Hagar's son could not die, for as a son of Abraham, he had a prophetic word over his life that he would inherit that land. God made sure that the child lived to see that prophetic word come to pass.

As long as you have a prophetic word from God waiting to be fulfilled in your life, you don't need to wonder if you are going to die in a plane crash or something. God's promises for you will always be fulfilled: "So is my word that goes out from my mouth: It will not return to me empty, but will accomplish what I desire and achieve the purpose for which I sent it" (Isaiah 55:11).

While Ishmael was special, God also sends His angels to those whom some might call "nobodies." Luke's gospel tells us that the angels visited a bunch of no-name shepherds to tell them about the good news of Jesus' birth (see Luke 2:8–20). It is very possible that those shepherds had been praying and asking God when the Messiah would come to deliver Israel from Rome. After all, that was the cry of most of the Israelites at that time. It would be plausible to say that God answered the shepherds by sending His angels to appear to them.

The gospel of John tells us that an angel came to heal the sick folks who sat praying by the pool of Bethesda:

> Now there is in Jerusalem by the Sheep Gate a pool, which is called in Hebrew, Bethesda, having five porches. In these lay a great multitude of sick people, blind, lame, paralyzed, waiting

for the moving of the water. For an angel went down at a certain time into the pool and stirred up the water; then whoever stepped in first, after the stirring of the water, was made well of whatever disease he had.

John 5:2–4 NKJV

Those people were not special. Much to the contrary, they were the outcasts, the sick and the marginalized, yet the angel of the Lord came to them. As in the past, God still sends His angels to answer our prayers today—the prayers of anyone who will call on His name, rich or poor, known or unknown: "But when we cried out to the LORD, he heard our cry and sent an angel" (Numbers 20:16).

There are many cases in the Bible when angels appeared to people. In some of these cases, the angel even talked to the person to communicate the will of God. In the New Testament we see many angelic visitations that were a clear result of answered prayers. It happened to Peter when the church prayed that he would be released from prison (see Acts 12:5–7). It happened to Zechariah, John the Baptist's father: "But the angel said to him: 'Do not be afraid, Zechariah; your prayer has been heard. Your wife Elizabeth will bear you a son, and you are to call him John'" (Luke 1:13). In both these Scriptures, God heard the cry of His people and sent His angels with the answer.

God still sends His angels to intervene in our favor today. He can and does send angels to answer our prayers, to bring us His messages, to reveal the interpretations of visions or dreams, and to give us His direction. As an angel told Daniel, "Do not be afraid, Daniel. Since the first day that you set your mind to gain understanding and to humble yourself before your God, your words were heard, and I have come in response to them" (Daniel 10:12 NIV).

51

Should We Pray to Angels?

The Bible clearly says that Jesus is our one and only, sufficient intercessor: "For there is one God, and one mediator between God and men, the man Christ Jesus" (1 Timothy 2:5 WEB). We should never pray to, nor try to "contact" or "speak" with, the angels. That would be crazy. Not even Jesus Himself called out to angels; He would have called on the Father to send them instead: "Do you think I cannot call on my Father, and he will at once put at my disposal more than twelve legions of angels?" (Matthew 26:53).

Jesus, the Son of God, came to earth as incarnate man. Though in essence He was and still is God, during His incarnation He also was 100 percent human. And as a man He taught us not to call on angels or pray to them ourselves. Rather, we should follow His example and pray to the Father, who will send His angels on our behalf.

If an angel appears to you and brings a message from God, then you can talk to the angel. We have a biblical basis to back that up; we can ask an angel questions regarding his message. In Judges 13, when the angel of the Lord appears to Manoah's wife and tells her she will conceive a boy and that he should be a Nazirite consecrated to the Lord, she runs and tells her husband about her encounter. Manoah then prays and asks God to send His angel again to teach them how to raise the boy. The Lord hears Manoah's prayer and sends the angel again, and then the three of them have a conversation about how these parents should raise Samson.

In this interesting story, you clearly see a man and woman talking to an angel. Yes, therefore, we can talk to angels when they appear to us. We can ask them questions. But there is *no* biblical precedent for invoking angels or calling out to them ourselves. We don't pray to them, and we don't ask them to show up or manifest themselves.

It is important to notice that Manoah did not pray to the angel and ask him to reappear. He prayed to the Lord and asked Him to send His angel again. Even in the Old Testament, the Israelites had an understanding that we are not supposed to pray to the angels—only to God. They knew that very well because of the first Commandment, which states that the people of Israel should have no other gods besides Jehovah. They understood that praying is something we should reserve to direct to God and God alone.

Biblically speaking, although we may ask angels questions when they appear, we should never directly invoke, cry out to, or pray to them, or ask them to manifest. I know I started this section with this verse, but let's make sure we get it: "For there is one God, and one mediator between God and men, the man Christ Jesus" (1 Timothy 2:5 WEB). We pray only to God, not to the angels.

All sorts of New Age types, and even some groups who claim to be Christian, teach their followers to pray to angels. Nevertheless, biblically speaking, we are not supposed to pray directly to angels. The Bible is very clear about that. We may pray to God the Father, God the Son (Jesus) or God the Holy Spirit. We understand that they are three different Persons of the same Godhead. In our prayers we can speak to any of them interchangeably, for they are the same God in nature and essence. But there is only one intercessor between God and man—Jesus Christ our Lord.

Just because God sends angels to talk to us does not mean that we should start trying to talk to angels. Just because God still sends angels to minister to His children does not mean that we should build a theology around it or start praying to them. Why should I ask something of an employee when I am a child of the Boss? I repeat, *we do not pray to angels.*

We don't need angels, saints or anyone else to intercede for us, because as God's children we can talk directly to our Father (see Romans 8:15). I am pretty sure that Jesus is more than able to handle the job of being our intercessor, without any help from deceased saints, Joseph, Mary or the angels. We already have the highest and greatest intercessor of the universe—Jesus Christ, our high priest: "It is Christ who died, yes rather, who was raised from the dead, who is at the right hand of God, who also makes intercession for us" (Romans 8:34 WEB).

I want to encourage you to pray to the Father and ask that He send His angels to bring you the answer you need. You have direct access to the Father, and your guardian angels see the face of your Father in heaven daily (see Matthew 18:10). You can therefore pray to the Father, and He will send angels to serve you and help you with your needs.

Visited by an Angel

After I finished speaking at a certain church on one of my ministry trips, a young lady approached me and asked for prayer for her dying mom. She briefly told me the story of how she and her brother had recently taken their mother to the hospital, where she was diagnosed with cancer. Many people in their church had visited and prayed for her, to no avail. She had lost over twenty pounds, and her prognosis was not good. One day they came back from the doctor with bad news, and it seemed like the next day the cancer had metastasized and she only had a couple of weeks of life left.

As I stood there listening to this young lady's story, a long prayer line formed behind her. She asked again if I could pray for her mom. I told her I would love to. She pulled up a cell phone and got her mother on the line. She had previously told her mother that she would call with me on the line to pray for healing, so her mother was already waiting expectantly. I prayed with her as the Holy Spirit led me. As I stood there and prayed over the phone,

I had a strong impression that I should ask the Father to send an angel to bring healing to her, so I did. I specifically asked the Father to send an angel to visit this woman and bring her healing to her.

We all felt a strong presence during that prayer. I finished praying, blessed her and said good-bye. Then I smiled at her daughter and asked, "Did you feel that?"

"Yes," she answered, with tears running down her eyes.

"Your mom will be okay. Do you believe it?" I asked.

"Yes, Pastor, I believe."

"Just call me Ed, and send my love to your mom. Tell her about what happened here and how we felt the Father's presence as we prayed for her."

"Okay, I will," she said as she turned around and left.

I carried on praying for people in my prayer line, still feeling that sweet presence. Many people were instantly healed.

A few days later, I was praying for people after I preached, as I normally do, when this woman came to thank me for praying for her and tell me that she was miraculously healed. I asked her of what, and she told me that, due to her cancer, the doctors had given her just a couple of weeks of life. But her daughter had me pray with her over the phone, and immediately after the prayer, an angel visited her and she was healed. I asked her to tell me how this wonderful healing happened. Here is the story as she related it to me:

> It was a cold, snowy night and I had two aunts visiting me. My oldest son was also with me. I told them you would pray with me over the phone, and they all prayed together in agreement with you. As you prayed for me, we all noticed this beautiful aroma of lilies. I hadn't seen any flowers in the house, but I asked if anyone had brought me flowers. They all shook their heads no. I am not a flower person, and there were no flowers in the house. I asked if everyone else could smell the lilies. My two aunts and my son all nodded affirmatively.

I was so puzzled by the scent of flowers that I decided to follow it with my nose to find out where it was coming from. My nose led me to the front door. When I opened it, I found this tall man standing on our doorstep. He was tall and had long, blond hair. He was wearing blue jeans and a long-sleeved white shirt and sandals. I thought the sandals were odd for the kind of weather we had, but I didn't think much more about it. His beautiful smile was inviting, and we felt a lot of peace just seeing him standing there.

"Hello there," I said to him, surprised to see someone standing on our doorstep.

"Peace be upon you and your household," he answered with a bright-white smile.

"Amen," I said to this tall, handsome stranger. "But who are you?" I asked, unaware of the puzzled look on my face, which my son later laughed about.

"My name is Raphael," said the tall stranger. "I'm a fellow servant of the Lord."

A few seconds went by as we all just stood there. My guests and I were dumbfounded by the peace, the presence of God and the sweet smell of lilies emanating from that man.

"May I come in?" he asked with a smile, his brown eyes sparkling under the snowy night.

"Of course. Oh my, where are my manners?" I clumsily walked back in and showed him the way. "It must be freezing out there," I said, pulling the lapel of my jacket together. It was indeed cold, but it didn't seem to bother this stranger. I got out of the way and opened my arm toward the living room. "Please, by all means, do come in."

"Thank you." He smiled and walked in, leaving that sweet fragrance of lilies lingering behind as he passed.

My son, my aunts and I stood there in the middle of the living room, respectfully staring at that intriguing young man. Later we talked about how weird it was that he was there and how we all had questions to ask about that unconventional visit.

But at the moment it happened, we were all so overwhelmed by the peace that walked into the house with him that we were suddenly speechless.

Well, almost everyone. I have this horrible habit of thinking with my tongue, and suddenly I heard myself saying, "What's the name of that cologne of yours, if you don't mind my asking?" I had a nervous smile on my face.

"You look sick; do you mind if I pray for you?" said Raphael, ignoring my silly question, his golden brows pressed together in a bunch.

I did look sick. In fact, I looked very sick, and I thought it was considerate of him to notice and offer to pray.

"No, I don't mind. In fact, I'd love it if you prayed for me."

I don't know how or why, but I knew that God had sent him to my home. I felt God's presence in his countenance. Not once did I have a negative or concerned thought about inviting a stranger inside. Instead, I felt a lot of peace, as if I'd always known him.

He came closer and placed his hands beside my head. He never touched me, just kept his hands one or two inches away from the sides of my head. But even without touching me, I felt this . . . the best way I can describe it is *energy*. It was this beautiful, warm energy, and I felt it come down from his hands onto my head and flow down all over my body. I then felt very light, like a feather. I felt so much peace; I could not even stay standing. I felt I was about to fall.

That's when he asked me, "Would you like to take a seat?"

I couldn't answer. I slowly nodded as I kept my eyes closed, overwhelmed by that nice, warm feeling of peace. I knew it was from God, and I welcomed it with every cell in my body. Finally, I managed to say yes. My son pulled out a chair and I sat down. Raphael, as he said his name was, kept his hands next to my head. I must have passed out, because I don't remember what happened next. All I remember is waking up the next day in my bed, feeling great.

My son later told me that I passed out under the power of God, with a look of great peace on my face and one single tear running down my right eye. I did not remember passing out. All I remember is sitting down and feeling this tremendous peace. Then I opened my eyes and it was morning. My son told me later that when I passed out, my aunts picked me up and placed me on my bed. When they came back to the living room, Raphael mentioned that he had to leave. My aunts insisted that he have some tea or coffee with them first, and he agreed. They sat down, and he drank some tea and started to tell them some beautiful healing testimonies. They said they could not hold back their tears as that sweet man shared those encouraging healing stories.

A couple of hours later, Raphael thanked my aunts for their hospitality and said he had to leave. They insisted that he stay with them because it was already late. He said he'd love to stay, but he really had to leave. They walked him to the door and watched as he disappeared under the fresh-falling snow.

The next day I was scheduled for some medical testing. My daughter (the one who called me and put you on the phone, Ed) came to pick me up to go to the hospital. My son also went with me, and he could not stop telling my daughter what had happened the night before. She asked me how I was feeling, and I told her I felt great.

We got to the hospital and I underwent the tests. After I got the results, I went to see my doctor. He was dumbfounded. There wasn't one speck of cancer in my body; it had all disappeared overnight. My doctor, who wasn't a believer, asked me what had happened. We told him the story about how you prayed for me over the phone and how a few minutes later Raphael came to the house and prayed for me, and then I fell, filled with peace, and woke up feeling great the next morning.

The doctor took a good look at my previous tests again (the ones that showed my body was filled with cancer) and compared them with the new tests I had just taken (which showed I had no cancer at all). Then he said, "Well, I don't understand how this is possible, but . . ." he paused for a second, looked at the tests again, looked at me and said, "the tests don't lie." He pressed his lips together and declared, "You are totally cancer free!"

My daughter wrapped her arms around me, crying. My son got up and hugged the doctor, saying, "Thank you, Doc!"

"Don't thank me," the doctor said, pushing his glasses up on his nose. "I honestly had nothing to do with it." He laughed nervously. "I don't know how this could be." He shook his head from side to side, raising his eyebrows. "The only thought that comes to my mind is that you've been visited by an angel."

Angels Bringing Healing

Do we have a biblical precedent for angels bringing healing? We already looked at one such precedent in chapter 1, when we talked about Jesus praying for the centurion's servant. I believe angels brought that servant his healing. I also mentioned earlier in this chapter what happened at the pool of Bethesda in John 5:2–4 (NKJV), where an angel would come stir the waters from time to time and the first person in after that would be healed. Let's look at verse 4 from that passage again: "*For an angel went down at a certain time into the pool and stirred up the water*; then whoever stepped in first, after the stirring of the water, was made well of whatever disease he had" (emphasis added).

I have heard people argue that there was no angel who came to stir the pool; such a thing was only what people believed was happening. That is the kind of thing you would expect a Bible skeptic to say. On the contrary, an angel definitely stirred up the waters of that pool. That is exactly what happened, because the Bible clearly states it in verse 4. In at least one of these wonderful angelic manifestations around the pool, a certain invalid tried to get down into the water, but someone else would get there before he did because of the condition of his legs. This man witnessed the stirring of the waters, presumably more than once, before Jesus healed him:

> Now a certain man was there who had an infirmity thirty-eight years. When Jesus saw him lying there, and knew that he already had been in that condition a long time, He said to him, "Do you want to be made well?"
>
> The sick man answered Him, "Sir, I have no man to put me into the pool when the water is stirred up; but while I am coming, another steps down before me."
>
> Jesus said to him, "Rise, take up your bed and walk." And immediately the man was made well, took up his bed, and walked.
>
> John 5:5–9 NKJV

I have had many experiences in which I prayed for people and felt the Holy Spirit prompting me to pray to the Father, asking Him to send His angels to bring aid, help or healing to someone. In many of these cases the Father opened my eyes to see in the spiritual realm, and I saw angels going to the place where the sick person was. In these moments I was so imbued with authority, anointing and faith that I would describe to other people the exact details of whatever place the sick person was in. If it was a room in a house, I would describe the color of the walls, the position of the window, where the person's bed was, what the decoration looked like, even little details like flower vases and pictures of people on the dressers. If the person was in a hospital room, God would show me the hospital room and I would describe it in great detail. The people I was praying with would be in tears immediately, confirming that what I saw was all true. I don't think I get those visions because I am more gifted or in any way more special than anyone. I believe that all those who have the Holy Spirit can move in the gifts of the Spirit.

I believe one of the reasons God gives us that revelatory gift is to increase faith in the hearts of those we are praying for or with. I remember one lady I prayed for in Destin, Florida, after one of my Friday Night Fire meetings. She came to me the next day and told me that when I had prayed with her the night before, I had looked at my watch and said, "Pay attention to what time it is right now; it's 11:45 p.m. Your son is being visited by an angel right now. . . ."

According to this lady, I went on to describe how her son was dressed, what he was doing, where he was and whom he was with. "He will puke out all the alcohol in his system," she said that I continued, "and he will receive the revelation that the people around him who are drugging themselves are not really his friends. He will come back home, and you will lead him to Jesus."

"It all happened exactly as you said," she told me. "He was where you said he would be, with the exact clothes on that you described and with the so-called friends you described." She continued with teary eyes, "Then, as he was poisoning himself with both legal and illegal drugs, suddenly he felt a strong conviction that he had to give his life to Jesus. He felt sick and puked out all the drugs and alcohol he had taken. All of a sudden he sobered up, looked around and realized those people were not really his friends. He felt an urge to come home. He came home about an hour later. I had just gotten home myself, arriving from our Friday Night Fire meeting. He walked straight toward me, knelt down, told me all that had happened and said, 'Mom, I want to give my life to Jesus.' We prayed together, and in tears he became born again. I kissed him and hugged him tight; I didn't care about the smell. I was radiant that my son was back and had given his life to the Lord.

At that exact moment, I remembered what you had said about the time. I held on to both his shoulders and asked, 'Son, do you remember what time that happened to you?' He told me yes, he did, because he had looked at his watch at the time to make sure I would be awake. I asked him what time his watch had said, and he answered, 'It was 11:45, Mom.'"

The Lord had answered our prayers by sending an angel to help that woman's son. I want to encourage you to believe that God sends angels with help and healing for His children. I want to encourage you to fill the place where you are right now with worship, call upon the name of the Lord in your heart and ask Him to send His holy angels with the answer to your prayers, in Jesus' name. Do it with all your heart; do it in faith. Ask the Holy Spirit to guide you and show you how to pray effectively. The Father will hear your cry and will send His angels to your aid.

6

Guardian Angels

See that you do not despise one of these little ones.
For I tell you that *their angels* in heaven always see
the face of my Father in heaven.

Matthew 18:10, emphasis added

You have angels assigned to you who are watching over your life. I am not talking about a mystical view of guardian angels. I am talking about a biblical view. Jesus said it Himself—the little ones have *their angels*. Jesus is stating clearly here that we have *our very own angels*. Matthew 18:10 is the best verse about the subject of guardian angels, especially because it comes from Jesus Himself. Not that we do not give divine weight to other Scriptures; we know that all Scripture is inspired by God (see 2 Timothy 3:16). But words that come from the mouth of Jesus carry an extra weight of authority, at least devotionally in our hearts. That is why so many Bibles print Jesus' words in red.

Notice that Jesus said *their angels*. The Greek text is transliterated *hoi aggeloi auton* and literally means "the angels of them." The Greek word *auton* here is a possessive pronoun.[1] Jesus clearly is stating that God has assigned angels to watch over us. Jesus also tells us that these angels *always* come before the face of the Father to receive His messages and gifts for us. What a beautiful thing to know that we have angels whom the Father has assigned to protect and watch over us. Not only that, but to know that our guardian angels always see the face of the Father in heaven on our behalf.

I do not believe our angels are meant to intercede for us. Jesus Christ is our all-sufficient intercessor (see 1 Timothy 2:5). Rather, among other things our angels are in our lives to guard us from the fallen angels and their attacks against our health, our relationships, our finances and every other area they can put their filthy hands on as they come to steal, kill and destroy (see John 10:10). Our angels are also meant to bring from the Father every good and perfect gift He sends us (see James 1:17). They also receive and bring us God's messages, which they sometimes communicate in visions, dreams, impressions, thoughts and other ways that they have to pass on His messages. The Bible says that they can even be disguised as visitors when they come to us. Hebrews 13:2 says that "some people have shown hospitality to angels without knowing it." Who knows? Maybe you have already talked to an angel. Maybe you have received one in your home without even knowing it.

Innumerable Angels

If God would give His only Son for us, why wouldn't He assign an angel to watch over each of us? There are angels enough in heaven for us all. In fact, their number is innumerable. My favorite Scripture on the subject of guardian angels is found in Acts 12, when an angel delivers Peter from prison. I love this passage. Peter is in jail, and the church is praying and asking

God to release him. An angel appears and tells Peter to get up. When he complies, the shackles fall from his wrists. The angel then tells Peter to follow him. The doors open before them as they walk out of the jail. The angel disappears, and Peter comes to the house where the other believers are gathered, praying for his release. They cannot believe he is at the door. Look what they say to the maid who answers his knock:

> When he knocked at the outer gate, a maid named Rhoda came to answer. On recognizing Peter's voice, she was so overjoyed that, instead of opening the gate, she ran in and announced that Peter was standing at the gate. They said to her, "You are out of your mind!" But she insisted that it was so. They said, *"It is his angel."* Meanwhile Peter continued knocking; and when they opened the gate, they saw him and were amazed. He motioned to them with his hand to be silent, and described for them how the Lord had brought him out of the prison.
>
> Acts 12:13–17 NRSV, emphasis added

I always wondered why the church thought it was Peter's angel standing outside. This text makes it clear that in the early Church, the first disciples believed that God had assigned an angel to watch over each of His children—a personal angel. Pay attention to verse 15, where the disciples say, "It is his angel." This verse clearly shows us that these early disciples also believed a person's angel looked like the person he was assigned to.

Are there angels enough for every person on earth? Daniel 7:10 (NRSV) says this: "A stream of fire issued and flowed out from his presence. A thousand thousands served him, and ten thousand times ten thousand stood attending him. The court sat in judgment, and the books were opened." The Bible does not give us an exact number of how many angels there are, but passages such as the one above give us the idea that there are a great many. In this particular text, it says "a thousand thousands" and "ten thousand times ten thousand." These numbers ought not be taken literally, because in Scripture these are a common Hebrew form for stating a vast number. But any way you take it, there are angels enough.

Jesus also gives us a hint about how many angels there are when He says, "Do you think that I cannot appeal to my Father, and he will at once send me more than twelve legions of angels?" (Matthew 26:53 NRSV). The term used in this text, *legion*, was a Roman military term that meant 6,000. Literally speaking, if we do the math, "twelve legions" would be 72,000. Jesus did not necessarily mean this statement literally either, because in the Bible we see reports of situations in which just one or two angels killed thousands of people (see Genesis 19; 2 Samuel 24:15–16; and 2 Kings 19:35). Imagine the damage that 72,000 angels would do! Jesus was not being literal by saying twelve legions; He was using a figure of speech to represent the vast number of angels at His disposal.

The Bible does not tell us specifically how many angels God created or how many angels there are in heaven, but all the passages that talk about this subject give us the idea that the angels are innumerable. As the author of Hebrews put it, "But you have come to Mount Zion and to the city of the living God, the heavenly Jerusalem, and to innumerable angels in festal gathering" (Hebrews 12:22 NRSV). Another translation of this verse says "to myriads of angels" (NASB). In that same translation, the term *myriad* also appears in Revelation 5:10–12: "Then I looked, and I heard the voice of many angels around the throne and the living creatures and the elders; and the number of them was *myriads of myriads*, and thousands of thousands" (emphasis added). The Greek word for *myriads* in both texts can be translated as "tens of thousands" and is used in the plural sense, meaning an innumerable amount.

Yes, there are enough angels in heaven to take care of each of us, so go ahead and ask God the Father to send you your own guardian angels to help you, protect you and bring you a miracle from His heavenly throne.

Tow Truck Angel

I want to close this chapter with an encouraging testimony my mother once told me. She was a woman of God. She and my dad raised my two sisters and me in church, teaching us to fear God from an early age. Mom always told us many stories about God's blessings and intervention. On many occasions, she would see angels.

It was not uncommon for Mom to say to me, "There's a man in white standing right over there; he's an angel of the Lord." She then would tell me what the angel was doing or why he had come. Sometimes she would see an angel interacting with somebody in church, and she would go up to that person and tell him or her what she saw the angel doing. Most of the time this would result in the person crying and confirming that all that my mother was saying made sense.

Sometimes Mom would see an angel bringing healing to someone who was bedridden or who had a terminal condition. Sure enough, the next day that person was healed. The following story is my mother's personal testimony about an angel who rescued my dad and her on a night when they were out in a rural area in the middle of nowhere. This story is in Mom's own words, as nearly as I remember them:

> It was about midnight. The church meeting we were at was so good that none of us wanted to leave, but we had to. After all, we all had things to do the next day. Tony and I said our good-byes to the church folks and got in our car. We were the last ones to leave. That was not a smart move. We had never been to that place before, and now that everyone was gone, we would have to find our way home all by ourselves.

I was glad we had decided to leave the children with their grandma. I wouldn't want them to be in the car this late on such a tiny, sinuous old dirt road in the middle of those dark woods. It had rained all day long and now we had to drive in zigzags, dodging the deep puddles; otherwise, we could get stuck in a mud trap. We had gotten stuck in the mud before—twice, actually. But both times were during the day, thank God, never at night. During the day there is always a good soul willing to stop to help, but at night it is a different story. Nobody is driving around late at night in the middle of the woods—well, unless you were some crazy Christians coming from a late-night prayer meeting. Anyhow, we'd better not get stuck or we would be in trouble.

I think it's amazing what happens when you keep thinking too much about something. I don't know if we keep thinking about something because God is trying to warn and prepare us for something that is about to happen, or if something happens because we can't stop thinking about it. Anyway, as I sat there trying to help Tony navigate through the puddles, suddenly the headlights shone on a puddle too big to avoid. Tony stopped the car, and it slid a few feet in the mud.

"Can we drive around it?" I asked.

"There's no way around it; it's just rocks, tall weed and the fences," Tony said. There were white wooden fences all along the road.

"Can we drive really close to the fence, over the weeds?" I asked.

"God only knows what's under those tall weeds," Tony gestured with his hand. "If we try to drive over them, we could hit a sharp rock and have a flat," he added, scratching his head.

"Do you think we can cross this giant puddle without getting stuck?" I asked, wiping my sweaty face with my hand.

"Well," Tony swatted a mosquito that had landed on his face, "I guess we're gonna have to find out." He stared at me, waiting for approval.

"Okay, go ahead, but go slowly," I said.

"Slow is worse; we should go fast and use the momentum of the car to get us through," he answered.

"If the others who left church before us made it, I guess we can make it, too," I said, and Tony nodded at me.

What we did not know was that the others had not taken the road we were on; they had gone back on a different one. For some reason we didn't get that memo, and there we were, having to drive on a medieval road in the middle of nowhere. Not only that, but now, to make things worse, we had to drive through the Loch Ness puddle.

I'm pretty sure by now you've already guessed what happened. Yes, we tried to go through it, and of course we got stuck.

"Dear Lord, I can't believe it!" I sighed the loudest sigh ever.

Tony kept trying to gas his way out of this huge mud trap. We could hear the wheels spinning under the muddy water. He got out of the car and got down knee-deep in the mud, trying to push the car out. It barely moved. My heart stared to race. Darkness surrounded us. Tony got back in the car and wiped his forehead with the handkerchief he always carried in his back pocket.

"What now?" I asked.

"There's nothing we can do. The car is stuck." He tried to catch his breath.

"Try it again," I said.

He did, but this time when he turned the key, nothing happened.

"Oh, bother," Tony said, "the engine won't start." He tried again, pumping his foot on the gas a few times. The car made that *chocking* sound and almost started a couple of times, but died again.

"I'm sorry," Tony said. "It won't start."

"Well, keep trying!" I said, overwhelmed by the thought of being stuck all night in the middle of nowhere.

"If I keep trying, it may be worse," he said, lowering his window.

"What do we do now?" I asked. I knew there was nothing we could do, but I asked anyway. You have to remember, this was a time before cell phones. And even if we had brought along a cell phone back then, I doubt it would've had any service in that place.

"Pray," Tony answered. "All we can do is pray."

So we did. We thanked God for that amazing revival meeting, for His sweet presence we had felt in that place and for His love, which we continued to feel in our hearts. We asked Him to send us help so we could get back to our children safe and sound.

"Amen," we said together. Everything was all so very quiet now. Only the crickets and a few frogs were brave enough to defy the silence of the night. A cold night breeze blew away the clouds, and the moonlight shone above us. I could smell the fresh aroma of grass and pine needles dancing along with the breeze. I thanked God for the moonlight and looked down outside the car. Mud, rocks and tall weeds surrounded us. The road cut right through the dense forest, the dark trees hidden under the dim moonlight.

Suddenly, when it seemed that we would have to spend the rest of the night in the car, we saw a pair of headlights shining behind us.

"Oh, thank You, Jesus!" I said. You know how thoughts race through our minds, right? Mine wasn't any different. I immediately thought, *Who could it be? Could it be somebody from church who left after we did? No, that couldn't be; we were the last ones to leave. Could it be the pastor taking someone to the hospital or answering an emergency call?*

I was still thinking of the possibilities when the headlights passed right by us. A wave of brown water hit the side of our car, rocking it a little. As the vehicle passed, we could see it was a big white truck. It drove right through the Loch Ness mud puddle as if it weren't even there and stopped right in front of our car.

"Turn on the headlights," I said to Tony.

He did. The headlights shone on the truck ahead. A tall, blond man dressed in a white shirt and white pants got out. He picked up a steel cable from a winch on the back of his truck and started tying it up to the front of our car.

"Don't just sit there," I elbowed Tony. "Go help the man."

He got out of the car to help, but it was too late. The tall stranger in white had already gotten back into his truck, so Tony jumped right back in ours and shut the door. The man started driving forward. His truck pulled our car out of that monster mud trap as if it were pulling a toy. Once we reached solid ground, the truck stopped. Tony got out of the car, unhooked the cable and placed the cable back on the winch of the truck. As soon as he did, the truck took off and disappeared in the darkness, beyond the reach of our headlights. Frowning and breathing hard, Tony got back in our car.

"What is it?" I asked.

"I should have asked him to wait to see if the engine starts," Tony said, staring at the wheel and holding it with both hands.

"Well, don't just sit there waiting for Christmas; turn the key!"

I never thought I would be so happy to hear the sound of that old engine. We drove away and tried to catch up with our rescuer to thank him, but his truck was gone. We couldn't even see his taillights.

"Tony, where is he?"

"I don't know. Maybe he turned at a crossroad," he said.

"We haven't passed by any crossroads yet," I said.

"Maybe he just drove away really fast." Tony shrugged his shoulders.

"Tony," I said, my eyes fixed on the road, "there are no wheel marks on the road ahead of us. It looks as if no car has passed by here in a long time."

Tony stopped the car. With the engine still running, he studied the dirt road ahead of us in the glare of our headlights.

"You're right!" he exclaimed. "The road is as clean as a baby's bottom."

We studied both sides of the road, but both sides were fenced private properties with no entrances off that road. We drove away without saying a word the rest of the way home. We arrived safely and parked in our garage. Tony turned off the engine, and I grabbed his hand. We both prayed and thanked God for sending His angel to help us in our time of need.

From that day on, I lived through the troubles of life with the confidence that in time of need, we could count on our guardian angel.

God commands our guardian angels to watch over us, save us and help us in time of need. "For the Scriptures say, 'He will order his angels to protect and guard you'" (Luke 4:10 NLT). Whenever you go through a storm in life, I want to encourage you to pray and ask the Father to send you your guardian angels to come to your aid. God did it for Jesus, and He did it for Daniel, Gideon, Joshua, Peter, my parents and thousands of other people around the world. He surely will do it for you.

7

They Come When We Worship

Now I have come to explain to you what will happen
to your people in the future, for the vision concerns
a time yet to come.

Daniel 10:14

I am thankful to the Lord for all the moments when He has
opened my eyes to see the angelic. I want to tell you about one
of these moments that is precious to me. It taught me a principle
that forever changed the way I do spiritual warfare.

As a young pastor I had researched and read everything out
there about spiritual warfare, which is a visual reality for us here
in Brazil. We grow up seeing people demonized in services, on
the street, on the bus, at work—anywhere. That is due to the
strong presence of African religions such as voodoo and macumba in this country. These religions came to Brazil with the
slaves the Portuguese brought here to work on the sugarcane

and coffee farms from the sixteen hundreds up through slavery's abolition in the nineteenth century.

I think one of the reasons why we Brazilians have so much faith in spiritual matters is that we grow up seeing fallen angels manifest and do their works. Once we get saved, it therefore is not hard for us to believe in the ministry of the holy angels.

Angels in the Living Room

The experience I am about to relate really did change the way I do spiritual warfare. It happened on a Friday night. My wife and I were exhausted after working twenty hours a day for over twenty days straight on a ministry trip. We got home and we were a wreck; all we wanted to do was take a hot shower, sink into bed and hibernate forever. But at three in the morning I got thirsty. I got up and went into the kitchen to drink some water. In my house, to get to the kitchen from our bedroom, you have to go through the living room. It is a big living room, and I walked like a zombie through it, trying not to trip and hit my chin on a coffee table or chair. The dim light of the full moon shone through the window as I reached the kitchen. I grabbed my glass of water and stood there sipping it.

Suddenly, I felt a presence in the living room. Not a good presence—a bad one. I felt the presence of the demonic. It was a hot and humid night, as are most of the nights in Rio, but all of a sudden the air got cold, really cold. A white mist came through the walls into the living room. I knew that was a sign of the demonic, so I prayed, *Father, open my eyes to see my enemies.*

As I prayed, the Lord opened my eyes and I saw the demons, six of them, standing in the middle of the living room. They looked like human-sized cobras, slithering their forked tongs in the air, their reptilian eyes filled with hatred and anger. At some point they noticed that I could see them, and they hissed at me like vicious snakes.

Oh, no! I said to myself. *I am not in the mood to fight demons right now. Lord, I'm so tired.*

I leaned down and placed my elbow on the kitchen cabinet and rested my head on the palm my hand. As I stood there trying to remember where I had left my anointing oil, I heard the Holy Spirit speak to me in a clear, yet gentle voice: *Just worship.*

Without questioning or thinking twice, that is what I did. I started worshiping the Father. I sang the first song that came into my head, "I Exalt Thee." I did not sing it out loud, because I did not want to wake my wife. I just whispered it, but in my heart I was shouting. By the time I started singing it for the second time, something amazing happened. Like a huge meteorite, this massive, broad-shouldered angel of light fell down into the middle of the living room. He hit the ground so hard that it literally trembled. I felt the ground vibrate as he landed powerfully.

This guardian angel straightened his shoulders and raised his chin. His beautiful white wings shone like marble shells over his head. He was about three feet taller than the demons. When the demons saw this angel, they all took a step back. As I continued to worship, another angel came down the same way. He looked very much like the first one. Now both of them stared down the demons, as the evil ones took another step back.

At that point I smiled. *I got it!* I thought to myself. *When I worship, the angels come and the demons flee. Awesome!* So I continued to worship, now excited about the angelic visitation. As I worshiped, another angel came down. Now there were three. I have had visions of angels battling demons with their swords, but on that night they did not have to fight at all. All they did was stare down the demons, who walked backward until they disappeared through the wall.

If I were a demon I would have left, too, because those angels looked as though they meant business. Their holy countenance pierced sharper and deeper than any sword I had ever seen. As the demons left through the walls, so did the cold mist that had filled the air.

I continued to sing, and the angels stood there in the middle of the living room, staring at me. I grabbed my glass of water and walked past them, whispering my song as I went back to my bedroom. As I passed each one of them, they nodded a long nod, with their sparkly hazel eyes fixed on me. I felt so honored and respected by them. As I sat down on my bed, I looked back through the open door and saw them jumping up into the air and flying through the roof, back into the heavenlies. What a great feeling I had in my heart; I felt like a worship warrior.

That night my understanding of my royal position as a son of the King of kings went up a notch. I lay down in bed, rested my head on my pillow and stared at the ceiling, imagining the stars up above. It took me a while to fall asleep. As I kept replaying that experience in my head, I realized that the angels were not saluting a mere human being; they were saluting a child of their Creator, a son of their Lord and King. They were saluting one of their princes.

After that night, never again did I have to spend a long time waging warfare against demons, nor did I spend any time trying to cast out devils. I learned the lesson that worship attracts angels and the angels do the cleanup for us. I also learned to use Randy Clark's 10-step deliverance model. I would assign those who felt called to deliverance ministry to take the demon-possessed to a separate room and work on their deliverance with them—not talking to the demons, but rather bringing a demonized person back to his or her senses and guiding the person, through repentance, into closing doors formerly opened to the demons.[1]

As time went on, I worked on that "worship warrior" concept a little more and deepened my understanding of the process. When I lived in London, I loved to go see the Changing of the Guard ceremony at Buckingham Palace. It is such a colorful, vibrant experience to see all those armed men perform their choreography. Whenever Queen Elizabeth makes a public appearance, she comes protected by the royal guard. In fact, military personnel protect any chief of state. The primary and ultimate task of a soldier is to protect the king. Even in chess you see how the king stands behind the pawn line, protected by his soldiers. Soldiers go before their king. What happens when we worship the Lord? When we wholeheartedly worship, He comes, often preceded by angels.

The Glory Cloud

We know that the Holy Spirit lives inside us, and in that sense God is with us always, fulfilling the promise Jesus made to His disciples that "surely I am with you always, to the very end of the age" (Matthew 28:20). But Jesus also said, "For where two or three gather in my name, there am I with them" (Matthew 18:20). Jesus is with us always, as He promised He would be. But He is also with us in a different manner when two or three are gathered in His name. These Scriptures show us that there are different manifestations of the presence of God. I do believe that when we worship, we attract a different manifestation of the presence of God. We see the same thing happening in 2 Chronicles 5:13–14, when Solomon consecrated the Temple:

> The trumpeters and musicians joined in unison to give praise and thanks to the LORD. Accompanied by trumpets, cymbals and other instruments, the singers raised their voices in praise to the LORD and sang: "He is good; his love endures forever."

Then the temple of the LORD was filled with the cloud, and the priests could not perform their service because of the cloud, for the glory of the LORD filled the temple of God.

Once I was preaching in a church in Bakersfield, California, when I felt I should lead the church into worship. We began to sing with all our hearts, and all of a sudden I saw these beautiful angels, about a dozen of them, come through the walls near the ceiling. They stood there, hands up, singing along with us as we wholeheartedly worshiped our Lord and Savior. As the church continued to worship, I was pumped by the vision of those angels. At that moment the Holy Spirit just fell on me, and I felt this rush of glory all over my body. I grabbed a Brazilian flag they had hanging amidst other flags on the podium and started to whack people with it and prophesy over them. As I did, people fell to the floor, totally drunk in the Spirit. Some were baptized in the Holy Spirit and spoke in tongues. Others were taken into visions.

The church kept worshiping, and the presence of God thickened in that place. I could feel His strong presence; it gave me goose bumps all over my body. I carried on whacking people with the Brazilian flag and prophesying over them. Suddenly, I felt someone pull me by the shirt. I was so focused on giving people prophetic words that I did not pay attention to the pulling at first. Then someone pulled my shirt again, this time so hard it almost knocked me off-balance. I turned to see who was pulling me, and it was Cherrie Kaylor, an awesome, anointed woman of God. I had met Cherrie and her husband, Michael, in Brazil in one of our healing crusades. Bright-eyed, she looked at me and pointed to the ceiling.

I looked up, and that is when I saw the glory cloud resting above us. It was a beautiful, visible white cloud. This time we were not seeing it with our spiritual eyes, but with our natural eyes, for the cloud of the glory of the Lord had manifested in the natural. Not everyone saw the angels, but everyone saw the cloud. Some people thought it was smoke coming from a smoke machine or perhaps from some sort of leak in the heating system. Later, the church leadership assured us that there was no leak in the building, and no smoke machine either. It really was the cloud of the presence of God. It was thick, like the clouds in the sky. It filled and covered the whole ceiling. It looked like bright white cotton candy. It moved and sparked with colorful lightning as it hovered over us. The lightning shone in all the colors of the rainbow inside the cloud. That night many people were baptized in the Holy Spirit, and many were healed.

I have only seen the physical glory cloud twice in my life so far. The second time was when I was preaching in a large church in Brazil. Again, I felt that I should lead the church in worship. As we worshiped, I saw a host of heavenly angels fly into the building. They joined us as we worshiped the Lord with all our hearts. As we continued, now joined by the angels, I saw this glory cloud manifest. It looked like a thick mist spreading all over the church. I felt the Holy Spirit telling me to have the church repeat this phrase ten times: "The Lord is good, and His love endures forever." I instructed the people to expect healing to manifest in their bodies as we repeated that declaration. I also told them that once we had finished saying it for the tenth time, we should all shout for joy to the Lord the loudest we had ever shouted in church before. Then everyone should check their bodies to see if they were healed. (I had done the same thing another time with Randy Clark in a crusade and the results were amazing, so I knew something good was about to happen.)

As we did all this, hundreds of people were healed all over the building. Deaf ears and blind eyes were opened, the lame walked, tumors disappeared, and people with all sorts of ailments were healed. A great joy took over the whole church as we all felt and saw the manifestation of the presence of God.

God literally inhabits or dwells in the midst of our praise. Psalm 22:3 (NKJV) says, "But You are holy, enthroned in the praises of Israel." When we praise the Lord and fill His house with praise and worship, He comes because our praise and worship is a pleasant house, a delightful dwelling place for His holy presence.

Why Angels Show Up for Worship

Why do angels show up when we worship? They come to prepare the way for their King. We already talked about how soldiers or a royal guard come before royalty to announce a king or queen's arrival. In the case of the presence of God manifesting, His angels come right before King Jesus manifests His holy presence in the midst of our worship. The angels prepare the way and announce the arrival of their Lord and King.

Recently, we did a spiritual swipe or cleanup in the area where we are planting a church here in Rio, Brazil. It is a very poor area that used to be the stage of the largest macumba center in the city. But God is so good that the center moved away right before we built our church building there. Nevertheless, macumba followers are still a strong presence in that area. They constantly leave their sacrifices of dead chickens and other offerings to their "gods" on the sidewalks at crossroads, and also on the sand at the beach.

Because of that, I gathered my disciples and the church people and told them, "Let's do a spiritual cleanup of this area." We met at the church, and I taught them the principle I had just learned about spiritual warfare. I told them that we would go about in the neighborhood with our guitars and anointing oil and we would worship, sing and praise God.

One of them asked, "What if a demon manifests on one of the neighbors?"

I answered, "God has given us authority, amen?"

"Amen," they echoed.

"So if demons manifest, you read them their rights."

At this point they looked at me, puzzled. "What rights?" one of them asked.

"Well, demons only have two rights—the right to remain silent, and the right to come out!"

They all laughed, and we went on with the cleanup. As we moved street by street, worshiping God and anointing the houses, the sidewalks and the beach, a host of angels came down and paraded with us, all around us. Some of us saw them and others did not, but we all felt the presence of God right there with us.

After that holy sweep, many of the neighbors came to church the next Sunday and asked what they should do to get saved. We led them to Christ, and that same night many people saw and heard angels singing and rejoicing over the church, celebrating the lives of those who had just been redeemed. "Likewise, I say to you, there is joy in the presence of the angels of God over one sinner who repents" (Luke 15:10 NKJV).

Who Let the Dogs Out?

I remember one time God opened my eyes to see an incredible sight when I was still a teenager living with my parents. It was three in the morning. I woke up hearing this weird noise of metal clashing against metal. The first thought that came to mind was that some kids were hitting our metal gate with a crowbar. Our two dogs were barking like crazy, which was unusual. Normally they did not bark unless there was someone at the gate, and that night they were barking and howling like a pack of wolves. I was afraid they would wake the neighbors. I got up, still sleepy, put on my slippers and went to check it out. I opened the window just enough to see what was causing the dogs so much distress. To my amazement, there they were—an angel and a demon— sword fighting in the middle of my front yard.

Fear struck me. Fear is the first natural human response to any angelic visualization. I wish I were not afraid when these things happen, but in most of my angelic encounters I have felt terrified. This is probably why most of the time when someone sees an angel in the Bible, the angel says, "Fear not." Of course, by the time the angel says that, it is already too late.

That night my knees started to shake involuntarily, a weird sensation. Have you ever had a body part move by itself without being able to control it? We are used to being in control of our body, and when a limb starts to move with a mind of its own, it is unsettling. I opened the window a little more and noticed that although the dogs would bark, they did not dare get close to the angelic beings. I say "angelic beings" because a demon is also an angel—a fallen angel, but an angel nonetheless. The dogs continued to bark and howl at the angels as they clashed swords.

I am so thankful that the Father opened my eyes to see in the spirit that night. It is a memory I cherish to this day. As a teenager challenged with having so many choices to make, that experience greatly strengthened me in my continued pursuit of the spiritual realm. The angel from God was tall, strong and broad-shouldered. He was different from others I had seen up to that point because he was wearing colorful armor, like a gladiator's. He did not have a helmet; he had long, curly golden locks that waved with every swing of his heavenly sword.

The demon, on the other hand, had only a rag tied around his waist and a sword, nothing else. The angel's sword was made of shiny light, whereas the demon's sword was made of pure darkness that seemed to suck the air around him into a vortex of panic and fear.

As I watched the two of them fight, I noticed that my dad had gotten out of bed and was standing right beside me, looking out the half-open window. He had his mouth open, and he raised his chin in order to look through the lower part of his prescription glasses.

"Can you see them?" I asked.

"Yeah . . ." he answered slowly. "Weird, huh?"

"I know!" I told him, excited that he could see the angels, too. "I've never seen anything like this."

My dad looked at my trembling knees and asked, "What's with the shakes?"

"What do you mean?" I asked.

He calmly pointed at my knees. "Your knees—they're shaking."

"Of course they're shaking! Aren't you afraid?" I asked.

"Afraid of what?" my dad asked as he leaned over the window. "There ain't nothing out there to be afraid of, except those two stupid dogs barking at the fence." He pressed his glasses against his nose with his index finger. "Hey, you!" he shouted at the dogs. Amazingly, the dogs stopped barking and looked at him. "Hush it!"

The dogs tilted their heads and went quiet for a second or two, but as they heard the clashing of the swords they turned back to the angelic duel and started barking again. Normally they would obey my dad and go inside their houses with their tails between their legs, but not that night. Not with the adrenaline rush they were getting from watching the angel fight that demon.

My dad turned around on his heels and went back into his bedroom, muttering, "Humph, crazy dogs . . ."

The next day, when I told my dad about the vision, he said I should have told him, but it was one of those moments when you don't think straight until it is over. At some point I had noticed that the angel of the Lord was having a tough time. The demon was pounding his dark blade at him so fast that all the angel could do was to hold up his own blade and defend himself. He was clearly losing his strength, and the blows were getting closer and closer to his face.

Father, what's going on? I prayed.

Instantly, I felt the Lord say, *This is a warrior angel. I sent him to watch over you and your family.*

But he's losing, I said.

Then I heard the Father say into my spirit, *Pray.*

I started praying in tongues like nobody's business. As I started to pray, the most incredible thing happened. The more I prayed, the stronger and bigger the warrior angel got. It was as if my prayers were somehow strengthening him. Theologically speaking, I think the best way to put it would be that God was listening to my prayers and strengthening His angel. But without getting into the theology, the fact was that the more I prayed, the stronger the angel became.

I raised both hands toward the angel of the Lord and continued to pray. As the angel got stronger, he started to fight back again. Now it was he who was bashing blow after blow of his sword of light against the demon. All the demon could do was hold his blade over his head and back down. As I continued to pray, the demon finally realized he was no match for the angel of the Lord. With a twist of his body, he became like a whirlwind of black smoke and flew up and away into the dark of the night.

After the demon had fled, the angel sheathed his sword and looked straight at me, nodding his head as if he knew I had something to do with his sudden victory. He then looked up, bent his knees and shot up into the starry night sky.

Musical Angels

In 2012, my wife and I started a church plant in the living room of our house in Rio, Brazil. A strong and tangible presence of

God marked our meetings from the start. We always shared words of knowledge for healing and then prayed for people at the end of the meetings. It was not long before our living room got too small and people were standing outside our door, hungry for more of God.

In one of these house meetings, I was playing my acoustic guitar as usual during our worship time. Back in the day, I was the only person playing an instrument. We did not have any other musicians. There were probably forty people crammed into our living room, and all we had was my acoustic guitar. I was playing a spontaneous song, and tears were rolling down my face over my big smile. The presence of God was so tangible that our hearts were melting before our Loved One. Most of the people in the room were either crying or bowing facedown before God. The beautiful smell of myrrh filled the air, a smell we had also experienced at other times when the Lord was with us.

As we continued in worship, suddenly we heard two distinct musical instruments playing along with my guitar. One sounded similar to a violin, and the other sounded like a cello. The interesting thing about this phenomenon is that all of us who were there that night heard it. No matter how many times you have such an experience, it is always very emotional. People started to freak out as we realized that the angels were playing music with us. After the first shock, we all rejoiced as we heard the wonderful chords they played as we sang to our Father in heaven.

This phenomenon recurred often in our house church meetings. The sounds varied at each meeting. Sometimes the sounds the angels played were more like classical string instruments such as violins and cellos. Other times the sounds were more like drum pads. We knew one thing for sure—those sounds were not coming from my acoustic guitar. It was not even plugged into anything; we were worshiping totally unplugged, and all we had was my old acoustic guitar and a cajón (a boxlike percussion instrument).

On two different occasions, we heard voices as well. They were very distinct, metallic-sounding voices that echoed our songs.

One certain night, the Father opened our eyes to see the musical angels who had joined us. I saw two of them dressed in white. They were standing outside our circle and singing along as we worshiped. I love when the Father shows the angels to more than one person, which provides such a powerful confirmation of what He is doing. One of our leaders came up and told me, with fear in his eyes, that he was seeing the angels in our meeting. He described them exactly as I was seeing them. When I told him that I could see them, too, he was overjoyed with the confirmation. I had him share the vision with the congregation, and we all rejoiced and thanked the Father for the angelic presence in our humble house church meeting.

That was three or four years ago. Since then, we have had many angelic visions and manifestations. Last May we got together at our church to record our live CD, and we started to smell the distinct aroma of myrrh again. When this happens, people start looking around for feathers, gold dust and precious stones, for those always seem to appear when angels manifest in the room. As we continued to rehearse for the recording, we could hear angels singing along. Because it has happened so often, our church already recognizes the angels' voices and instruments. But this time it was so loud, so awesome and so beautiful that one group of people who were hearing it were awestruck and threw themselves on the ground, shouting and crying. We have also had a lot of new members join our church recently. When the newbies heard the angels, they thought it was some keyboard effect, or a synthesizer or pads. They did not notice that we had none of those things around to use on our CD, only guitars and drums. It was interesting to watch the newbies' puzzled looks as they tried to understand what the people on the floor were freaking out about. After all, our songs were good, but they were not so good that we were at the point of throwing ourselves on the floor! (Just to clarify, this happened on the second day of the rehearsal and unfortunately was not reflected in the recording itself.)

Angels Singing Our Songs

One time, the chief priests and teachers of the law heard children shouting "Hosanna to the Son of David" in the Temple courts. Indignant, they asked Jesus (whose presence and miracles were the cause of the uproar) if He heard what the children were saying. Jesus answered them, "Yes, . . . have you never read, 'From the lips of children and infants you, Lord, have called forth your praise'?" (Matthew 21:16). Another translation puts it this way: "Out of the mouth of babes and nursing infants You have perfected praise" (NKJV). Perfected praise rises from the lips of God's children. It is interesting to me that when angels come to worship with us, they do not bring another song. They come to sing along with our songs.

I have heard so many people pray, "O Lord, take us up to heaven so we can hear what the angels are singing and repeat it in our worship here on earth." I have also heard worship leaders say that they were taken up to heaven in a vision and saw the angels worshiping God, and they long to remember the songs they heard so they can minister them to the Church. I remember one worship leader who even made a big deal about his songs by saying that he had heard them in heaven, and he encouraged his church to sing what was being sung in heaven. But let's not confuse Jesus' intention with His prayer, "on earth as it is in heaven." Jesus was not talking about worship when He said that; He was talking about God's will: "Our Father in heaven . . . your will be done, on earth as it is in heaven" (Matthew 6:9–10). The will of the Father is what is supposed to come down from heaven to earth, not the worship. Not everything must be from heaven to earth. Our prayers, for example, rise from earth to heaven. Our worship also rises from earth to heaven. While I appreciate the intention of that leader, I would like to propose that it is the angels who long to hear *our* songs and sing them in heaven.

Angels worship the One who stands before them as their Creator. We human believers worship the One who lives *inside* us as our Father. There is a big difference. (I know that technically, it is the Holy Spirit who lives inside us. But we also know that as part of the Trinity, the Father, Son and Holy Spirit are one and the same in essence, so it is not wrong to say that the Father and Jesus also live inside us. That is why Jesus said in Matthew 28:20 that He is with us always.) We are the children of God, and the Bible says that one day we will judge angels (see 1 Corinthians 6:3). When the angels look to us in the spirit, they see their Creator living inside us. The very One who created them and gave them their power and glory lives inside us. And as children of the Creator, we also are creative. All creativity comes from our Father, and He has filled us with it. I want to propose that as children of God, we are far more creative than the angels. It should come as no surprise to us, therefore, that the angels would want to come down and hear our songs, sing along with us and perhaps even bring our songs with them back to heaven to minister them to God.

If you are involved with worship in your church at any level, I want to encourage you to bring this new perspective to your worship team: Besides singing other people's compositions, sit together as children of God and create your own worship songs. Let your love and passion for the Father overflow through your own mouth, in your own words. May you express such passionate worship that the heavenly hosts will want to come down to earth to learn it, so they can bring it up to heaven and minister it to their Creator.

Heaven 9-1-1

Revelation 8:3 says, "Another angel, who had a golden censer, came and stood at the altar. He was given much incense to offer, with the prayers of all God's people, on the golden altar in front of the throne." When you feel that there might be a war going on in the spirit, pray. Ask the Father to send more troops and strengthen the ones who are already in the battle.

At one point Daniel prayed and fasted for 21 days. On the first day he started praying, God heard his prayers and sent an angel with a message for him. But a great demon, the prince of Persia, resisted the angel of the Lord and would not allow him to come to Daniel. On the twenty-first day, God sent Michael to help the other angel of the Lord fight. Michael overcame the resistance the demonic prince of Persia had imposed, and then Daniel could receive the message from God (see Daniel 10).

I wonder what would have happened if Daniel had quit praying and fasting on the twentieth day and had gone back to his normal life, thinking, *Well, at least I tried.* Do not give up your prayer and intercession, no matter what happens. And remember that the angels come when we worship. Keep believing, praying and worshiping, and God will send His angels to you with your answer, your healing, your financial breakthrough, your miracle or whatever it is that you need and have been asking Him for in prayer. He is faithful and just, and He is a good Father, but you must do your part. Never give up crying out to God, no matter how long it takes. The man at the pool of Bethesda had been there, believing and praying, for 38 years. He never quit asking the Lord to send an angel with his healing. God honored his faith and perseverance by sending Jesus Himself to heal him.

Do not faint. Do not give up. God is for you and not against you. He will surely send you His angels to bring you the answer to your prayers.

8

They Come When We Pray

> As I was praying, Gabriel, whom I had seen in the
> earlier vision, came swiftly to me at the time of the
> evening sacrifice.
>
> Daniel 9:21 NLT

My wife and I were at the Vancouver airport in Canada, going
through immigration to get into the United States, when something out of the ordinary happened. We had flown literally
hundreds of times into and out of the United States, and we
had never had any problems with immigration. But this time,
as we stood in line to be interviewed and have our passports
checked, I noticed that the immigration officer stared at us
for two seconds too long. I also noticed that he was wearing
a big turban on his head and a large, snake-shaped gold ring
on his right pinkie. For some reason that ring caught my eye
and made me feel weird. All of a sudden my gut churned, and
I immediately started praying in tongues.

My wife, who was standing in line right in front of me, turned and said, "What are you praying in tongues for?"

I was not praying loudly; in fact, I was barely whispering. But my wife was born equipped with the most amazing pair of ears ever.

"No reason," I answered.

"You never pray in tongues for no reason," she replied.

She was right, but I had not wanted to worry her with a slight impression.

"So tell me," she insisted, "why are you praying in tongues?"

"Don't stare at him, but see the guy with the gold ring?" I discreetly raised my eyebrows toward the guy.

"Yeah." She started staring at him, not so discreetly.

"Stop staring!" I whispered a little louder.

"I'm not staring!" She tried not to stare, to no avail.

"He's about to give us trouble," I whispered.

"How do you know?" she whispered back, still staring.

"I don't know; I just know," I said.

"What are you praying for?" she asked.

"I am praying for help."

"You're making me nervous," she said.

"That's why I told you it was nothing in the first place. I didn't want you to worry about it."

"Well, too late!" She frowned at me.

"Maybe it's nothing; maybe I got it wrong."

I said that to calm her down, but it did not work. Our turn came and we walked up to the immigration officer with the big turban and the funny ring. He looked at our passports, asked a couple of routine questions, then told us to go through a little blue door to our right.

Unhappy and worried about being late for our flight, we went through the little blue door. Then we went through the little metallic gray door, and it led us into a room filled with other foreigners, most of them Middle Easterners. Another immigration officer took our passports and told us to sit down and wait for them to call our names.

It is interesting to me how, more often than we are aware of, God uses signs and gives us clues about what is going on. As we sat there waiting for them to call our names, something interesting happened that I took as another sign. Standing in one of the booths and talking to an immigration officer was Jensen Ackles, a Canadian actor famous for his role as Dean Winchester on the CW series *Supernatural*. By now we were sure this was spiritual warfare, so we engaged in intercessory prayer. The TV star did not stay more than five minutes before off he went with a smile. We were not so lucky. Forty minutes went by. Dani made me go up to one of the officers a few times to ask what was going on. I did it, even though I felt in my spirit that nothing we did in the natural would help. Yet it made her feel better, so I did it, always praying in tongues under my breath.

A few feet from our seats, in front of one of the booths, there was a dark-skinned man dressed in a white Middle Eastern robe. He was being interviewed by this immigration officer and trying to convince the officer that his turban was a religious symbol. He said it would be a violation of his civil rights if they forced him to remove it. That argument did him no good. After all the complaining and arguing, he still had to unwrap the turban from his head.

Fifty minutes went by. Now Dani was really nervous. Our flight was scheduled to leave in fifteen minutes. All of a sudden, when all hope of catching that flight seemed lost, I saw lightning hit the middle of that big room—*bam!* There he was, an angel. He landed so hard that he bent his knees and touched the ground with one hand. I must have made a face, because Dani immediately squeezed my arm.

"What?" she asked, her eyebrows shooting up.

"What, what?" I asked with my eyes fixed on the being of pure light.

"What are you seeing?" she asked.

"How do you know I'm seeing something?" I asked her.

"Because you have that look on your face."

"What look?"

"That silly look you have on your face when you see an angel," she replied, curious.

Meanwhile, the angel straightened up, looked at the offices and booths around him and then dashed so fast into one of the booths that all I could see was a blazing white blur.

"It's an angel, isn't it?" Dani asked, boggy eyed.

"It was an angel," I smiled, "but now he's gone."

"What did he say? What did he do?" she asked, grabbing my arm really tight.

I looked at her and smirked. "They should release us any minute now," I said, sure of it now that we had our own immigration angel.

"Mr. and Mrs. Rocha." A loud voice came from one of the booths.

I grabbed Dani's hand. "C'mon, let's go."

We sat in front of the friendly, red-haired officer in the booth as he said, "Sorry for the inconvenience." He stamped our passports with a big smile. "Here you go. Have a nice trip."

"What about our luggage?" Dani asked, while I slit my eyes and stared at the officer's deep-blue eyes.

"They're already in the plane, ma'am." He stood up and handed us our passports with another smile. This was the nicest immigration officer I had ever met. "We don't want you to miss your flight, do we?"

Dani grabbed the passports and thanked him. Then she pulled me by the hand, running. "C'mon, Ed, don't just stand there! We're late."

We ran through the exit door, and Dani let go of my arm. I stuck my head back through the door to catch one last glimpse of that angel, and there he was again, standing right in the middle of the room. He looked at me and smiled, his dimples slitting his eyes. Then in a split second, he looked up again. Like lightning, he jumped up and zapped through the ceiling.

"What's wrong with you?" Dani grabbed me and got me running again. "We're going to miss our flight!"

I tried to keep up with her hurried steps as I smiled and told her, "No, we're not." It all brought Psalm 34:7 to mind: "The angel of the LORD encamps around those who fear him, and he delivers them."

Angelic Mechanic

I grew up knowing that the angels come in answer to the prayers we direct to the Father. Pastor Silvio, one of my first pastors, taught us that. He often had his spiritual eyes open to see in the spirit realm, and he would tell us where angels were in the church building and what they were doing. Most of the time, we would get confirmations in the natural about what he would tell us in the spiritual.

I used to ask him, "Pastor Silvio, pray for me to see the angels the way you do!"

"Not yet," he would tell me.

"Why?" I would ask insistently.

"The question, young man," he would say, looking straightforward as if I were not there, "is not *why*, but *when*." He always said it with a smirk.

"Okay," I would say, looking down. "When?"

"Soon, my young boy, soon," he would always reply.

Eventually, he did pray for me to see the angels, and I will get to that story later. But as an example of how the angels come when we pray, I want to tell you about one time when Pastor Silvio told our congregation to pray because he was seeing in the spirit realm that one of our church elders was stuck in the middle of nowhere, with the hood of his car open over a fuming engine. The church started to pray. We prayed for about five or ten minutes, and then Pastor Silvio told us he was seeing an angel coming to this elder's aid. He described the angel and how he touched the engine and fixed it. This was in a time before cell phones, so we could not call our elder brother to tell him we were praying for him, nor could we ask where he was so we could send help. We had to depend more on God back in those days.

As we continued in prayer, Pastor Silvio told us, "Pray that Brother Samuel will try to start the engine again and it will work."

We prayed probably for another minute or so, and then Pastor Silvio interrupted us again to say, "Done! He turned the key, and the car started. He's on his way to church now."

We continued our worship service, and half an hour later our elder brother arrived, sweaty and with his tie knot loose and pulled to the side. A couple of the more curious church members went up to greet him and ask him what had happened.

When Pastor Silvio saw Brother Samuel walking into the building of our Pentecostal Baptist church, he promptly said in the microphone, "Brother Samuel, come and tell the church what happened to you and how the Lord delivered you from harm."

Brother Samuel came onto the stage, and one of the sound guys handed him a microphone. "Thank you, Pastor," he said as he tried to fix his fine silver hair and his tie. "First of all, I want to greet the church . . ." he started to say in our church's customary greeting. The kids finished it for him: ". . . with the abounding grace and peace of the Lord." They did not say it loudly or disrespectfully, but quietly and in a joking manner, smiling and elbowing each other as they did. For some reason, almost everyone who ever spoke in the microphone of that church always said the same words before speaking. It was always the same greeting, as if it were part of church doctrine or something.

"I was on the way to church, coming from my house in my neck of the woods," Brother Samuel continued, "and I don't have to tell you where I live, cuz most of y'all already know that." He smiled. "So I was driving to church on this dirty road, when suddenly the—"

"*Ahem!*" Pastor Silvio cleared his throat loudly, interrupting Brother Samuel in the middle of what he knew was about to come out as a profanity. With his blind cockeye closed in a slit and his one good eye wide open, Pastor raised his brow and leaned forward to make sure Brother Samuel could tell he was staring at him. A few distinguishable, yet not too loud, teen giggles were heard among the congregation.

"Well, that is, I mean," Brother Samuel continued, "the *blessed* car engine just gave way on me."

"Then how did you get here?" asked Pastor Silvio, raising his chin with the customary assurance he always had about his visions.

"I suddenly felt this cold wind blow by me," Brother Samuel answered. "It brought shivers to my spine—but good shivers. I felt the presence of God."

"And what did you do then?" asked Pastor Silvio, smiling.

"I tried to start the engine again, and to my surprise, it worked!"

"Brother Samuel, now let me tell you what you didn't know." Pastor Silvio told him what had just happened in the spirit realm—how the church had prayed and God had sent an angel from heaven to fix his car. Pastor spoke with his usual and sometimes seemingly arrogant posture, except that he was not arrogant. He was just proud of what the Lord had done. He always gave all the glory to God and never took any for himself. He was a very humble man who rejoiced in whatever God did, and he always seemed proud of God.

Brother Samuel cried when he heard Pastor's part of the story, and he raised his hands up to God in a gesture of thanksgiving. Then he went back to his seat as the people in the church got up and started to clap their hands in praise, thanking God for sending His angels in our aid.

Pastor Silvio was a great man of God. He could see in the spirit realm, and he was a loving and beloved pastor. Physically speaking, though, let's just say he was not so charming. It is interesting how God so often does not care about the appearance of the people He chooses. David is a good example of this, or better yet, David's brother Eliab. God did not choose Eliab as king even though he was tall and handsome. God does not choose based on looks, for looks do not impress Him. Hearts do. Look at 1 Samuel 16:6–7:

> When they arrived, Samuel saw Eliab and thought, "Surely the LORD's anointed stands here before the LORD."
> But the LORD said to Samuel, "Do not consider his appearance or his height, for I have rejected him. The LORD does not look at the things people look at. People look at the outward appearance, but the LORD looks at the heart."

God does not choose us according to looks; He chooses us according to our hearts. So many times, it is through the weak and the feeble that God shows Himself strong. Good thing for Pastor Silvio; otherwise, he never would have been chosen. Pastor Silvio was a Danny DeVito look-alike with strabismus in his blind eye, which made him look cross-eyed. You could never tell if he was looking at you or at something else. He always wore the same thing—a white shirt under a gray or light-blue suit, always with a matching tie. Along with all that, he constantly wore a funny half-smile on his face. And despite the fact that he was a Pentecostal preacher, there was no emphasis on healing at his church. He believed God could heal if He wanted to, but Pastor Silvio did not pray for healing, nor did he teach on it. Because of that, nobody had ever prayed for his strabismus, and it was never healed.

It is funny when you think about it—William Seymour, the anointed man whom God used in the famous Azusa Street Revival, was also blind in one eye. But Pastor Silvio's disability did not seem to bother him at all. If you asked him about it, he would tell you that not seeing out of one eye actually helped him see in the spirit realm. He was an amazing man, and I was always anxious to see in the spirit realm, as he did. I was thankful that he taught us about how angels come when we pray.

Keys to the Angelic

Intercession is key to releasing the angelic. In the passage I started this chapter with, Daniel 9:21, we see that Daniel was praying when the angel came to him. And back in chapter 5, we looked at how God sent His angel to deliver Peter from prison *because* the church was praying for him (see Acts 12).

In Luke 1:11–13 we see another example of God sending His angel in answer to prayer. Zechariah and Elizabeth were praying for a son, and the Lord sent an angel to announce that their prayer had been answered:

> While Zechariah was in the sanctuary, an angel of the Lord appeared to him, standing to the right of the incense altar. Zechariah was shaken and overwhelmed with fear when he saw him. But the angel said, "Don't be afraid, Zechariah! God has heard your prayer."

Gabriel appeared to Zechariah and told him that he had come in answer to their prayer (see verse 19). Elizabeth then got pregnant with John the Baptist, and Gabriel also appeared to Mary to announce the birth of Jesus.

Expectation is another key to unlocking angelic manifestations. Once you walk around with the understanding that you are not alone—that you are surrounded by God's angels, who are here to serve and protect you—I promise you that your path will light up with activities in the angelic realm.

Again, I encourage you to pray and ask the Father to send His angels with the answers to your prayers. In Psalm 34:7, the Bible says the angels of the Lord *camp* around us. The original language of this verse says that they establish residence around us. Wherever you go, your angels go with you, to protect you and bless you with all the gifts sent by the Father. Know that God loves you, and know that He uses His angels as messengers. Acknowledge and be aware of their presence around you, and thank the Father for sending them. They come when we pray.

9

They Come Bringing Gifts

Create in me a clean heart, O God, and put a new
and right spirit within me.

Psalm 51:10 NRSV

I love to receive gifts, and I have been given many good ones. But angels brought me the greatest gifts I have ever received. Of course, I am not counting the gifts of the Holy Spirit; those are incomparably precious spiritual gifts, without which I don't think I would have made it in my spiritual journey. Rather, I am talking about material gifts. Seven angels once lined up in front of me and brought me material gifts. Before I tell you more about that, let me say that these gifts were not in the natural realm when they were given; they were in the spirit realm. But later they manifested in the natural. Isn't that everything concerning how faith works? First you believe, and then what you believed for manifests in the natural: "Now faith is confidence in what we hope for and assurance about what we do not see" (Hebrews 11:1).

It was a beautiful Saturday morning. The skies were blue, and the fresh smell of pine was in the air. I had been asked to translate for an American speaker, and I was getting ready to step up on the platform. We were in a city called Petropolis, close to Rio de Janeiro, Brazil. We had a team of about forty North Americans with us. There was a beloved elderly lady from Canada on the team, an intercessor named Mary Smith. Mary has since gone to be with the Lord, but I remember the kindness and gentleness in her eyes. She came up to me that morning and said, "Brother Ed, would you mind if we pray for you before you translate?"

"Yes, please, by all means." I smiled, placing my hands in "receiving mode."

Mary gently touched my hands and prayed, "Dear heavenly Father, please come and touch Ed as he goes up to translate. Fill him with Your Spirit. Send Your angels to minister to him."

The moment she said that, I saw this ten-foot-tall angel coming from behind her, straight toward me. He had a long white robe as bright as the sun. He held a huge sword of pure light that looked like a star in his hand. He also had a serious look on his face. This angel shoveled his star sword right into my belly. As he did, I felt this huge impact. It was as if a big truck had hit me. The impact threw me backward about ten feet, and I landed flat on my back on the concrete floor. I was down there for four hours. To this day, I think of it as the most incredible, godly, mystic angelic experience I have ever had. God ministered many things to me that night, things that changed me forever.

It was on that very peculiar morning that I experienced trichotomy,[1] becoming intensely aware of my body, soul and spirit. I had always believed that we are a composite of these three distinct components, but for the very first time I actually experienced it. It is one thing to have head knowledge of something,

101

but another thing to experience it with our senses. As I looked down during that experience, I saw that from my waist up there were three of me. Immediately, the "me" on the right started to laugh—not only laughing, but this part was hitting my thigh really hard and having a blast. I knew it was my spirit because he was having the time of his—or should I say my—life.

As soon as my spirit started to blast away in laughter, the "me" on my left, which I knew was my soul, started to complain. I knew this part was my soul because I could tell that the thoughts were coming from the head on the left. They were not happy thoughts—not at all. My soul was saying, *Stop this nonsense right now! This is not proper. We're supposed to go up there and translate for the speaker. It's our duty, our job. What are people going to think?* To this my spirit replied with a burst of laughter, as if he had heard the most amazing joke ever.

Then, right in the middle of these two other parts was my body. I knew this part was my body because it was where the pain was coming from. Plain, simple pain. My belly was painfully burning hot where the angel's sword had entered it, and all my tummy muscles were contracting. After that morning, my abdominal muscles hurt for three days. I think I did a thousand abs that day, because every time my spirit laughed, my abdomen would contract as if I were in labor. I had the worst case of spiritual contractions I have ever seen.

My heart also burned with the most exquisite kind of pain. It hurt so much that I thought I would die. I actually prayed, *God, I know this is from You, but if You don't stop it, I'm afraid my heart won't handle it. My chest and heart are aching so much that I think I'll have a heart attack.*

The Father answered with, *I am giving you a new heart.*

Then I saw this hand come and stick all these fingers into my heart and rip it open. I physically felt a burning pain as it happened. Honestly, I really did think I would die. As I felt that terrible, burning, heart-attack sensation in my body, my spirit burst into even more laughter.

What's so funny? my soul asked in this crazy internal dialogue—or should I say monologue, since my spirit did not reply with a word? All he did was laugh for joy, while my body cried in pain.

After the Father ripped my heart open, there was an empty spot inside me and new flesh grew in and filled the hollow. I could feel my physical heart burning and itching. It itched so badly that I tried to scratch it by actually rubbing my chest hard. I clenched my teeth as hot tears of pain poured from my eyes.

"There, there," said Mary. "Bless him, Lord."

I glanced at her and saw that she seemed to be enjoying all of this.

"Yes . . ." she continued to pray, "more, Lord."

"No! No more, no more!" I said.

"Yes, dear," said Mary. "Let the Father do His work in you."

"But you don't understand," I managed to say through clenched teeth. "It hurts really bad!"

"Fear not. Just trust Him," she replied.

As I saw this bright white hand touching my heart and filling the hollow with new flesh, I said, *God, I think You're going to kill me.*

In reply to that, I clearly heard the Father say, *Good; I need you dead.*

Somehow I knew what the Father meant. It was not that He was going to kill me in the flesh, but that I needed to die to myself—to my old dreams and desires. He wanted me to live for Him—for His vision, His calling and His destiny for my life.

Yes, Lord, I replied, *I'm Yours.* I said it through my clenched teeth. *Do to me as You please.*

I am giving you a new heart, the Father replied, *for the old one cannot handle the things I am about to do in and through you.*

After this intense experience, I did feel different. I felt a new love and compassion for the lost, to an extent that I had never felt before. And after this encounter it became easier for me to endure more pain, betrayal, frustration and so many other things that afflict the human heart. Afterward, I had to make some choices and deal with some people and circumstances that I don't believe I would have been able to handle had the Father not given me a new heart.

Isn't that what the Lord promised He would do? He told Israel, "I will give you a new heart and put a new spirit in you; I will remove from you your heart of stone and give you a heart of flesh" (Ezekiel 36:26). We are the new Israel, so this prophetic word also applies to us. God wants to give us a new heart—a heart that beats in unison with His own.

The First Angel: A Window to Heaven

Right after the experience of receiving a new heart from the Father, seven angels came and lined up to bring me gifts from Him. I cannot tell you about all seven; that would take a while due to how extensive the experience was. But I want to share three of them here.

The first angel came to me and said, "Look up."

As I looked up, I saw a window. It was the most beautiful window I had ever seen. Its design was intricate and delicate. It looked fine and sophisticated, yet organic and simple. It contained many colors, but three seemed to prevail: gold, blue and a shade of emerald.

The angel then said, "This is the gift I bring you. The Father has opened this window over you. It is an open heaven. You have it over you wherever you go."

Before I go any further in explaining this gift, let me say that we all have an open heaven over us wherever we go. When

Jesus died on the cross, the veil of the Temple was torn in two: "At that moment the curtain of the temple was torn in two from top to bottom. The earth shook, the rocks split and the tombs broke open. The bodies of many holy people who had died were raised to life" (Matthew 27:51–52). Christ paid our debt in full, and what happened to the veil signified the way that His sacrifice guaranteed us full access to God's presence once again.

Formerly, the veil had separated the people from the holy of holies—a sacred place in the Tabernacle of Moses where the Ark of the Covenant originally sat. There, the presence of God would manifest and He would speak only to the high priest. Four pillars that held up the veil of the covering defined the holy of holies area. Behind the veil sat the Ark of the Covenant (see Exodus 26:31–33). According to Mosaic Law, after sanctifying himself, the high priest could enter the holy of holies once a year, during the festival of Yom Kippur, to intercede for the people. The veil symbolized the separation sin had caused between mankind and God. When Jesus took our sins on the cross, He canceled that separation, and God supernaturally rent the veil to establish a natural sign of the redemption. The *Scofield Reference Bible Commentary* puts it this way:

> The veil which was rent was the veil which divided the holy place into which the priests entered from the holy of holies into which only the high priest might enter on the day of atonement, (See Scofield "Exodus 26:31") [Leviticus 16:1–30]. The rending of that veil, which was a type of the human body of Christ [Hebrews 10:20] signified that a "new and living way" was opened for all believers into the very presence of God with no other sacrifice or priesthood save Christ's.[2]

When the apostle Paul talks about Jesus paying for our sins, he compares it to a debt we all had in the spirit realm:

> He made you alive together with Him, having forgiven us all our transgressions, having canceled out the certificate of debt consisting of decrees against us, which was hostile to us; and He has taken it out of the way, having nailed it to the cross.

> Colossians 2:13–14 NASB

The moment Jesus died on the cross for us, the certificate of debt we had concerning our sin was canceled. Jesus paid it in full; therefore, all those who believe in Him have eternal life. They have direct access to the throne of God in heaven and access to the power, ministry and manifestation of the Holy Spirit in and through their lives.

I knew all that in my mind. I had learned the fundamental concepts fully in seminary. Nevertheless, I only had head knowledge of it. I had not yet tapped into the supernatural power of God, except for a few experiences that happened despite me and not because of me. I believe the window the angel brought me that afternoon was not a window itself, but the awareness that a window was there, made available to me. I had already been a pastor for ten years and I had my theology in place theoretically, but I was not living the supernatural life Jesus purchased for us on the cross.

Let me put it this way: Even though I was a charismatic believer, all the charismatic experiences I had had up to that point only affected my own life. I was not bringing any change to anyone around me. I was not making the world a better place through supernatural means, by the power of the Holy Spirit. Up to that point in my life, I could count on the fingers of one hand how many healings had taken place when I prayed for the sick. And it was not for lack of praying for them; I had always believed in healing. I could also count on the fingers of one hand how many angels I had seen and how many supernatural experiences I had had. After that day, all that changed. The window the angel brought me was a supernatural revelation of my sonship and my spiritual birthright to the power of the cross.

After the gift of the window, I started seeing more and more people healed when I prayed. As I continued to pursue revelation and anointing for healing, the number of people who were healed increased. Today, ten years after that experience, it is not uncommon for me to speak at meetings where most of the people I pray for get healed. I have had a couple of meetings where all the people who came asking for prayer got healed, and I am talking a couple hundred people. Today, the number of deaf people healed when I prayed for them is currently 178 and counting. And 10 blind eyes have been opened, 22 people have been healed of cancer, 25 people have had growths and cysts disappear, two paralyzed people have walked out of their wheelchairs, and much more. Before my experience with the angel who brought me that window and the revelation thereof, I would have been surprised if anyone had gotten healed when I prayed. Today, I am really surprised if someone I pray for is *not* healed.[3]

What this window does to me is that, the moment I start to worship, my awareness of the active presence of God and the ministry of angels increases exponentially. So does my faith for the supernatural manifestations of heaven in our meetings. Perhaps it is not so much a window to heaven, but rather a window in my discernment, a window in my understanding and in my expectation of what God is able to do. I have learned that expectation and faith are key elements that unlock the supernatural presence and manifestation of God in the midst of His people. In special moments such as these, I have seen angels, feathers, gold dust and even the physical manifestation of the Shekinah glory cloud. Because so many people have questions about—or even question—such manifestations, we will have an interesting discussion about them in chapters 10 and 11. But as I shared previously, twice this manifestation of the Shekinah glory cloud was visible in the natural to everyone in the building.

I have also had several people around the world come to me in meetings and tell me that they actually have seen this open window of heaven over my head when I worship. The supernatural is indeed released through this window, or the revelation of it, if you will. Thinking about the window activates my faith, and I can connect to the unseen realm where the angels abide. As we connect with heaven in worship, we attract the manifest presence of God. Angels come down to dance and worship with us, and then all heaven breaks loose.

The Second Angel: Gold Coins

The second angel came to me and said, "Stretch forth your hand." When I did, he placed three gold coins in the palm of my hand. They were shiny, round and big, as big as the palm of my hand, and they were made of pure gold. The angel looked at me and said, "Heavenly provision."

When I saw the three coins in my hand, I pressed my eyebrows together and with a puppy face said, "Only three?"

The angel smiled, picked up another gold coin and placed it alongside the others.

I looked at the four coins, and with a happy smile I said, "May I have more, please?"

Again the angel gently smiled at me and placed another gold coin in my hand. That went on two more times, and then when he placed the seventh big, shiny gold coin in my hand I said, "There you go, seven is a good number. Thank you."

The angel smiled at me again and left. Up to that time, my wife and I had always been tight on money. We both always worked hard and always had good jobs, but for some reason money was always an issue. After that visitation, we started seeing more and more supernatural provision in our finances. Money would appear in our bank account. We would find money on the street. People would come give us money. They would stick envelopes with cash or checks in our pockets and tell us, "The Lord told me to give you this." Ever since we had that angelic visitation, never again did we lack anything.

Before that experience, many nights we would go to bed wishing we could eat something we could not afford to buy. After the angel gave me the gold coins, never again did we crave something we could not afford. Never again did we need to pay rent and live on someone else's property. The Lord blessed us with our own home and a beach house—both fully paid for.

Before we had that experience, we could not afford a good car. We always had a broken-down ride that often left us stuck in the middle of nowhere. If you live in a first-world, developed country, cars are not a big issue. A lot of people who don't have good salaries still have a good car. But by way of comparison, in Brazil cars are three to ten times more expensive than in America, so most people have cheap old cars. After the angelic visitation with the gold coins, never again did we get stuck in the rain in a broken-down old car. Today, I have the car I always dreamed of.

After that visitation by the angel with the coins, God's supernatural provision became abundant in our lives. I finally understood what it means to be royalty, to be the son of the King. I understood that my provision did not come from my job, but from my Father in heaven.

The Third Angel: A Red Book

The third angel came to me bringing a red booklet. On the booklet's cover was written *Nations* in gold letters—not just the color, but actual gold, as if someone had melted gold and used it as ink. As a missionary in Europe I had visited twelve countries, but at that point when the angels came, I had not been out of Brazil for eight years straight. I did not even have a passport anymore. After that visitation my wife and I felt called to travel to the United States to speak and minister to North American churches. Right then it was extremely hard for a Brazilian to get a visa to the United States. I spoke to many people with solid backgrounds, well-accomplished business-men and pastors alike, who had had their visas denied by the American embassy. Then I learned that since my grandfather was from Portugal, I could apply for Portuguese citizenship as a means of attaining a passport.

European citizens do not need visas to get into North Amer-ica, Canada or any country in the European Union, so I started the process of becoming a Portuguese citizen. After a long and tiring application process, the Portuguese consulate denied my request. I was so frustrated. I had really believed that the pass-port the angel had shown me was a Portuguese passport. I prayed and told Father God, *I've done my part. I've done all I could in the natural. Now it's up to You.* Then I rested, knowing that when God wanted me to travel to the nations, He would make a way. I totally forgot about it, and a few months later, on my birthday, Dada God gave me a beautiful birthday gift. To my surprise, that morning I got a letter out of the blue from the Portuguese consulate. It said that they had reviewed my case and granted me citizenship.

When I showed the approval letter to my wife, she said, "What? But I thought they had denied it. These guys don't simply go back on something like that for no reason. Did you go reapply?"

"Nope," I answered with a big smile.

"Then what happened?" she asked.

"God happened." I winked.

Now I can travel without a visa to any country in North America and Europe. And since that day, that is exactly what I have been doing, answering the Lord's call on our lives and spreading the Brazilian revival fire to the nations. And guess what the European Union passport looks like? That's right—red, with golden letters, just as I had seen when the third angel came. "Ask me, and I will make the nations your inheritance, the ends of the earth your possession" (Psalm 2:8).

I believe God wants to surprise us with good gifts. He dispatches His angels to bring us blessings, healings, gifts and miracles, according to our needs. I believe He wants to send His angels to visit you and bring you the answer to your prayers. I encourage you to open your mind and heart to the reality of angelic ministry. Pray to the Father to send you His holy angels with the miracle and provision you need. Above all, ask Him to give you the revelations that you may still need to be able to advance in the Kingdom calling and destiny He has for you.

10

Seeing Angels

For in him all things were created: things in heaven
and on earth, visible and invisible, whether thrones
or powers or rulers or authorities; all things have
been created through him and for him.

Colossians 1:16

There is an entire spiritual reality surrounding us. In the natural
we are unable to experience this parallel reality through our five
senses, but that can be changed. The Bible is filled with accounts
of angelic sightings and interactions between angels and people.
In Genesis 16 we read the saga of Hagar and her son, Ishmael,
which we talked about briefly in chapter 4. They are about to die
in the desert when she hears the angel of the Lord speaking to her:

God heard the lad crying; and the angel of God called to Hagar
from heaven and said to her, "What is the matter with you,
Hagar? Do not fear, for God has heard the voice of the lad
where he is. Arise, lift up the lad, and hold him by the hand,
for I will make a great nation of him." Then God opened her

eyes and she saw a well of water; and she went and filled the skin with water and gave the lad a drink.

Genesis 21:17–19 NASB

After the angel spoke, God opened Hagar's eyes to see the well of water that saved them from certain death. The Bible gives numerous accounts of people's eyes being opened to see angels.

Unless God opens our eyes, we cannot see angels. That was God's design in creation, and it was a touch of mastery, as is every one of His touches. Imagine how crazy the world would be if humans could see angels the way we see each other. Surely, that would change considerably our perception of the world and how history happened. Furthermore, it would affect Judgment Day, because ignorance would no longer be an option. People would have no excuse for not embracing God. Faith would no longer be a requirement, either, for you would not need to believe in the unseen since everyone would naturally see it. The consequences of this kind of interference in human nature and history are unimaginable. It was crucial, essential and fundamental, therefore, that humans not see—and remain unable to see—the angelic.

String Theory

The deeper scientists go into quantum physics and other similar studies about the fabric of the universe, the closer they get to the unseen parallel realm of the angels. In 1954, a young Princeton University doctoral candidate named Hugh Everett III came up with a radical idea: There exist parallel universes exactly like our universe, and these universes are all related to ours. Recently, string theory enthusiasts have been popularizing the concept of parallel realities.

In physics, string theory replaces the smallest particles of our reality with one-dimensional strings. A string looks just like an ordinary particle, except that its mass, charge and other properties are determined by the vibrational state of the string. The vibration of the string determines whether it is part of this reality or another parallel reality.

More and more scientists are coming to the conclusion that other so-called "realities" exist parallel to ours. In his books *The Elegant Universe* (W. W. Norton, 2010) and *The Fabric of the Cosmos* (Vintage, 2005), Dr. Brian Greene tackles the existence of multiple parallel realities. Of course, these scientists always see things from a scientific and not a spiritual perspective. If one of the string theory scientists ever saw or communicated with an angel, he or she would probably call the angel an extraterrestrial being from another parallel dimension, or something similar to that, but never a spiritual being sent by God.

Do Angels Have Bodies?

Another theory is that as ethereal beings without real bodies, angels are made of particles and therefore do not possess mass. That is the popular belief because, first of all, most people think the spiritual realm is not a real realm in terms of the laws of physics. Second, their notion that angels can fly, go through walls (as happened when an angel rescued Peter from jail in Acts 12) and perform other impossible tasks enforces the popular belief that angels are not made of real matter with real mass, but are of a spiritual, and therefore ethereal, composition consisting of pure energy.

That is indeed a possibility we cannot dismiss. The Bible is not specific about the composition of angelic bodies on a molecular level. It could well be true that angels are made of pure energy, so the way they show themselves in the Bible could be merely a metaphorical and symbolic representation of their essence.

Some people believe that angels have sometimes been caught on camera in their pure ethereal forms, which many people commonly refer to as *orbs*. An orb would be a metaphysical manifestation of the ethereal essence of an angel. If this theory of angels being purely ethereal is true, then all the apparitions, encounters, materializations, manifestations and visualizations of angels where people have perceived them to have humanlike bodies simply have been anthropomorphism. In other words, the people involved have attributed human traits, emotions and intentions to nonhuman entities. Psychologists consider anthropomorphism one of our innate human tendencies.

Further, if this ethereal being theory is right, then angels neither wear clothing nor carry swords. All biblical reports of angels wearing garments and holding instruments such as scrolls and swords would merely be symbolic imagery angels used to facilitate their communication with humans. A verse that seems to support this theory is Luke 24:39, where Jesus says, "Behold My hands and My feet, that it is I Myself. Handle Me and see, for a *spirit does not have flesh and bones* as you see I have" (NKJV, emphasis added).

On the other hand, the apostle Paul seems to declare that heavenly creatures do have bodies, just as earthly creatures do:

> All flesh is not the same flesh, but there is one flesh of men, and another flesh of beasts, and another flesh of birds, and another of fish. There are also heavenly bodies and earthly bodies, but the glory of the heavenly is one, and the glory of the earthly is another.
>
> 1 Corinthians 15:39–40 NASB

One way or another, what we know for sure is that angels are real and occupy a single space in time. They can go through walls, fly at tremendous speeds and perform other supernatural actions because they are not bound to the natural physical laws of our realm, such as gravity and inertia. They can bend and even break those laws and behave in supernatural ways that are impossible for anyone or anything in our human realm. People have seen them as men wearing robes, eating food, handling swords and holding censers and other objects (for instance, see Genesis 3:24; 19:1–3; Numbers 22:23; Matthew 28:3; Acts 10:30; Revelation 8:3, 6).

In his sermon titled "Image and Likeness of God," John W. Ritenbaugh, founding pastor of the Church of the Great God headquartered in Fort Mill, South Carolina, said about this, "The angels ate. Can we assume they had the other bodily parts necessary for consuming a meal—stomach, intestines? It is difficult to determine how far we can carry this, but they did eat human food."[1]

No one can tell for sure whether angels have permanent physical bodies in the spiritual realm that occasionally manifest in our realm, or whether they have ethereal bodies and occasionally assume human form. Asserting one way or another would be a mere assumption. The Bible gives us grounds to believe either way. Angels may have physical bodies in their heavenly dimension that occasionally materialize in ours, or they may consist purely of energy and occasionally assume human shape and form. Both ideas are biblically plausible. Either way, the fact remains that humans cannot see angels unless the angels want to be seen and God allows us to see them.

How We See Angels

Angels are spiritual beings from another dimension different from ours, or another reality or realm parallel to ours. As we just talked about, we can only speculate about whether the angels' celestial bodies have mass or consist of pure energy. What we do know, however, is that our natural eyes were not designed to see them.

The very back of the human eye is lined with a layer called the retina, which acts very much like the film of a camera. It is a membrane containing photoreceptor nerve cells that line the inside back wall of the eye. These photoreceptor cells capture the reflected light emanating from whatever object we focus on, and they change the light rays into electrical impulses and send them to our visual cortex (a large area in the back of our brain that is responsible for processing visual information). That is where the object's image is formed.

In other words, our eyes were created to see light, and we therefore cannot see in the absence of light. Not only that, but we can only see what we call the visible spectrum of light. Since angels are not from our natural reality, they do not reflect the visible spectrum of light that the human eye can see, which makes them invisible to us. Even if an angel is standing right in front of you, there is nothing for your retina to capture and send to your brain to form the angel's image. Naturally speaking, that is why we typically cannot see angels.

When humans do see angelic manifestations, we can sort them into four categories that we get from their biblical appearances:

1. *Materialization*—God changes the molecular structure of the angels so that they can interact with our realm and our human senses can perceive them.[2]
2. *Visualization*—God gives people the temporary supernatural ability to see the angels in their own natural state in the spiritual realm.
3. *Visions*—God shows someone visions of angels. In this case it could involve a prophetic insight of times to come, such as in the apostle John's visions in Revelation.
4. *Dreams*—God sends angels to speak to people in their dreams and to bring messages to His children. A good example of this is when an angel visited Joseph in a dream. The angel tells him not to forsake Mary and assures him of the divine nature of the baby she carried within.

Instances of these four categories happen interchangeably within the scope of the Bible, and I categorize each biblical instance for your convenience in chapter 12. Since the first two cases, *materialization* and *visualization*, are the most common biblical means of interaction with angels and are more relevant to our discussion here, let's look at examples of each. These examples will help us better understand the nature of such angelic manifestations.

Two examples of *materialization* occurred when angels appeared to Abraham in Genesis 18 and Lot in Genesis 19. In Lot's case, many people in Sodom not only saw but also heard the angels. Another proof of the angels' materialization was that they ate food and touched both objects and people (see Genesis 18:8; 19:16).[3] These are clear cases of angelic manifestations where the angels were given the ability to interact with our physical world. Throughout Scriptures there are many other cases such as these, which prove that angels do at times have physical matter that can manifest in our realm of existence.

An example of *visualization* occurred when Elisha's servant saw an angelic host surrounding them (see 2 Kings 6:8–17). At first, only Elisha was seeing the angels. His servant and the enemy army were present, but they could not see the angelic host. It was only after Elisha asked the Lord to open his servant's eyes that the man was able to see the heavenly army. This is a classic case of visualization. The angels did not materialize, or everyone present would have seen them. God opened Elisha's eyes, and later his servant's eyes, to see what otherwise could not be seen.

Concerning how we see angels in real-time angelic appearances, we conclude that it can only happen if they physically materialize in our realm of reality and reflect light that our retinas can capture. In that case, anyone present at the time could see them. Of course, God could also open our eyes at specific moments so that we could see angels who have not materialized in our realm of reality.

Photogenic Angels

Sometimes our retinas capture the image of an angel and we can actually see one, and sometimes they don't. The same is true of cameras. Sometimes God allows people to capture the image of an angel on film (or digitally these days), and sometimes it doesn't happen. When it does happen, though, it is clear that angels are amazingly photogenic. They truly are a sight to see!

In my iPhone, I carry around the image of a beautiful angel who was captured on film. Let me tell you how it happened. In chapter 7 I told you about Pastor Silvio, one of my first pastors, and how he often saw into the spirit realm. Angels frequently were present in his church services. I also told you that I was always asking him to pray for me, so that I would be able to see in the spirit realm, as he did. The day finally came when he laid hands on me and prayed for my eyes to be opened to see the angels. I had just turned eighteen, and I was so excited! I could not wait to start seeing angels. Pastor Silvio also prayed for a few other youth from our church, young men who were really hungry for more of God. After that impartation, we often would see angels come and help during a service while Pastor Silvio was preaching. Sometimes the angels would show up in actual pictures, just as we had described them. I loved it when that happened, because it showed us that we were not going crazy.

One time when we were having water baptisms in the river, we suddenly started to tremble and praise God in a mixture of ecstasy and fear because we witnessed the presence of a beautiful angel standing in the middle of the river, right beside the elders who were baptizing the new converts. There were three of us young men there who could see the angel, and we all were smiling and trembling. I think we were experiencing that same mixture of awe and fear the shepherds must have felt in Luke 2:9: "An angel of the Lord appeared to them, and the glory of the Lord shone around them, and they were terrified." Those people at the river who could not see in the spirit did notice our excitement, and they asked us what was going on.

"There's an angel right there in the water!" we told the folks around us on the riverbank.

"Where?" they asked.

"Right there!" we pointed to him. "Right by the folks who are being baptized."

"What's the angel like?" they asked.

"He's got big broad shoulders and a big golden book in his hand." With fear and trembling we described what we saw in detail as well as we could. "He's standing in the middle of the river, with water all the way up to his waist, just like the people who are being baptized."

We told them about the angel's beautiful white garment and his belt that looked like a golden rope tied around his waist. We told them about his long golden hair with locks that hung below his shoulders. We told them about the golden book in his hands. We took turns describing what we saw. While one of us was telling people all about it, the others were speaking in tongues and glorifying the Lord. Besides being surprised, excited and scared all at the same time at the sight of the angel, above everything else we were so happy that we all were seeing the same thing together, which was a major confirmation for the others around us that the vision was real.

I hate to say this because it makes me realize how old I am becoming, although I guess time passes quickly for everyone. In those days we did not have digital cameras. (One day you will be old, too, and you will be telling your kids that you used to hear music from a silver disc called a CD, and they will laugh at you.) Back then we used film in our cameras—you know, old-school film that we had to take in somewhere for development. It would take a few days to have pictures developed before we could see them. People whose family members had been baptized in the river that day had taken pictures of the baptism and had them developed. For our enjoyment, that angel we had seen appeared in a few of the shots taken by different cameras from different angles. The angel looked exactly the way we had described him on the afternoon of the baptism. The pictures were a major confirmation for the church that we kids really were seeing angels. The pictures generated such frenzy at the church, in fact, that people from other churches started coming to our meetings just to see the angel pictures.

Pastor Silvio was not happy about the pictures. In fact, he seemed mad about them. "You're not supposed to believe because you see something in pictures!" he shouted over the microphone one Sunday. "You should believe in angels because the Bible says they're real." He slapped the pulpit for emphasis. "Our faith should not depend on pictures or any other evidence of the supernatural, but on the Bible and the Bible alone!"

But it did not matter how much Pastor Silvio reminded our church not to overvalue the pictures. People continued to have copies of them developed, and they even made photocopies and spread them around.

One day Pastor Silvio decided to collect all the pictures and get rid of them. "I want you all to surrender your angel pictures to me—all of them," he demanded. (There were many angelic manifestations at that church besides the one at the baptism, and many of these manifestations had been caught on film.) "I don't want any of these pictures circling around anymore," he continued. "I don't want your faith to rest on a picture, but on the Word of God."

Pastor Silvio preached about this a few Sundays in a row. He said the same thing over and over again, Sunday after Sunday, until he had collected all the pictures of angels. People gave them to him in obedience, thinking he would give the pictures back to them later, after everyone's fascination with the images died down. He never did.

I think it is a shame that Pastor Silvio took such a radical measure. I agree that our faith must not rest on signs and wonders, but there is nothing wrong with them. Actually, Jesus said that many people would not believe unless they saw signs (see John 4:48). Think about Thomas, who only believed after he saw the sign of Jesus' nail marks and pierced side. God uses signs and wonders to strengthen our faith and glorify His name. It is such a shame that nobody told that to Pastor Silvio. He kept asking the congregation to give him all the photographs. As a result, all the angel pictures from those days are gone. Pastor Silvio took them somewhere and hid them away forever.

Well, okay, maybe not all of them. One picture managed to survive, and I happen to have a copy of it that I carry on my iPhone. The angel in it is amazingly beautiful and photogenic, and I treasure the image dearly. I have shown it to a few friends, and perhaps one day, if you happen to come to one of my meetings, I could show it to you.

The Seers

Many people who call themselves *seers* claim they have received a permanent gift of spiritual vision and can see the angels all the time. I respectfully believe they are mistaken. I don't think the human mind could handle the amount of revelation that kind of gift would bring. Nor could anyone cope with the effects of continuous exposure to the angels' activities in the heavenly realms. Besides, I believe God has a purpose for everything He does, and I cannot see the purpose of someone seeing angels 24/7.

Imagine yourself one morning in the comfort of your home, using the toilet, when suddenly *boom*, you see an angel standing there with his arms crossed in the corner of the bathroom.

Imagine yourself one day walking on the sidewalk of a busy downtown street, when suddenly an angel passes right by you and you become so distracted watching him that you walk straight in front of a large bus.

Look what happened to Balaam: "Then the LORD opened the eyes of Balaam, and he saw the angel of the LORD standing in the way, and his sword drawn in his hand: and he bowed down his head, and fell flat on his face" (Numbers 22:31 KJV). This is the kind of thing that would keep happening to someone who was seeing angels continually. The angels are always going back and forth to establish the will of God on earth, and they are so awesomely beautiful and astonishing that no matter how many times you saw them, they would always have to remind you to "fear not."

There is no biblical basis to sustain someone having a permanent gift of seeing the angels. In the New Testament the Holy Spirit gives us nine spiritual gifts, and these gifts are permanent and irrevocable (see 1 Corinthians 12; Romans 11:29). Seeing in the spirit is not one of these gifts. What the Bible clearly teaches is that God occasionally allows people to see into the spiritual realm in order to accomplish His divine purposes. God opened the spiritual eyes of many people in the Bible so that they could see the angelic, but they did not continue to see in the spiritual realm indefinitely.

A Prayer for Visualization

Angels are real. They are all around us. Ask the Father to open your eyes so you can see them. God showed angels to Abraham, Jacob, Moses, Elijah, Elisha, Elisha's servant, Gideon, Peter and also common folk such as Cornelius in Acts 10 and the shepherd boys who came to see baby Jesus in Luke 2. Even today, thousands of Christians around the world have reported incredible accounts of their encounters with angels. I invite you to continue digging deeper into the supernatural reality, where God wants to expand your experience and intimacy with Him and His angelical beings. To get to the deep waters of the open sea, you have to lose sight of the shore. Open your mind and heart to see the angels, and God will open your eyes.

I want to pray a prayer for visualization for you, just as Elisha did for his servant. When the prophet prayed, his servant's eyes were opened to see the angels of the Lord surrounding them. The Father can open your spiritual eyes right now, too, so you can see His holy angels according to His divine purposes for your life.

If you have kept reading this book up to this point, then I am pretty sure that you believe in angels. But you may not be sure if God will open *your eyes* to see them, for three reasons:

1. You may feel you don't deserve it.
2. You may feel you are not active enough in the Kingdom of God for Him to open your eyes to see angels.
3. You may think you live a pretty regular life without much engagement in heaven's agenda, so there is no need for God to send you an angel.

My answers to these three thoughts are:

1. Nobody deserves to see angels; it is not something you earn by works. We have to be careful not to transform God's *charismata* into *worksomata*. That is to say, we should not change His gifts of grace into something we can achieve or earn. God does not grant open vision to those who deserve it. It has nothing to do with our ability, rank, status, works, position or anything like that.
2. God has opened the eyes of many people who were not doing anything for Him. He has even opened the eyes of

those who were working against Him, such as the prophet Balaam, who was sent to prophesy against the people of Israel (see Numbers 22:31).

3. You are God's child, and He greatly loves and cherishes you. He has a specific calling and purpose for your life. There are angels assigned to watch over you who daily see the Father's face on your behalf. You might just as well see them.

If you believe in angels and want to see them, if you are desperate for the things of God and are hungry for more, if you earnestly seek spiritual gifts and really want open vision, I want you to read this prayer with faith in your heart:

Heavenly Father, thank You for the gift of life, and thank You for Your angels. Thank You for these pages that I am holding in my hands right now. Thank You for sowing hunger for more of Your supernatural realm in my heart. Thank You for my desire to see the deeper things of the Spirit. O Father, I pray that You would hear my prayer right now, just as You heard the prayer of your son Elisha, and that You would open my eyes so that the angelic realm will become a greater reality in my life. Father God, bless me with the gift of open vision. Reveal the ways and things of the Spirit to me. Open my eyes to see Your holy angels, so that my faith in Your goodness may rise, and so that I may witness Your love and care in every situation in which You send Your angels to protect, serve and strengthen me. Open my eyes, Lord, I pray. Open my eyes to see Your holy heavenly warriors, and may this gift of open vision bring glory to You, Father, in Jesus' name, Amen.

11

Feathers

"Unless you people see signs and wonders, you will
never believe."

Jesus, in John 4:48

All around the world, in places where people are crying out
for revival, feathers are manifesting out of thin air, floating all
around the congregations and landing gently on people or on
the floor of the revival grounds where they are meeting. Before
I share my personal take on this manifestation, I want to share
with you what Kris Vallotton,[1] a leader at Bethel Church in
Redding, California, has to say about it:

> I don't think we have taken more ridicule for anything than [for]
> gold dust and feathers. It all began one day while someone was
> preaching, and these tiny white feathers started falling from the
> ceiling in the sanctuary. It wasn't raining feathers or anything
> like that (people tell tales), but they were very obviously there

and easily seen. At first no one said anything. We all thought there were birds in the AC ducts or something.

Then other leaders began to report the same phenomena happening in their churches. Our maintenance staff investigated the bird theory. No birds, feathers, or nests were discovered anywhere in the ductwork or the ceiling. It also started to happen in people's homes. It always happens when we are talking about the things of God. The phenomena tend to come and go. No one at Bethel has ever preached on feathers (that I know of), but at times it is nearly impossible not to mention them when we are teaching because several of them are falling right in front of the pulpit all at once. I have witnessed this myself a couple hundred times in several different buildings.

I have had several skeptics ask me "if I believe in feathers." LOL! I want to say "no!" because I understand that I sound like a kook, but I have seen them with my own eyes.[2]

The Bible is filled with accounts of the supernatural or spiritual realm manifesting into the natural in different ways. In fact, I intended to include in this chapter some other manifestations such as gold dust, gold teeth and precious gemstones that materialize, but there is so much to say about feathers that they warranted a chapter of their own. (We will look at some of the other manifestations in the next chapter.) Jesus Himself is the greatest reference of the Kingdom of heaven manifesting on earth. In Him, the *logos* Word of God became flesh. His body was not conceived naturally; Mary became pregnant by the supernatural power of the Holy Spirit. If we are okay with God supernaturally manifesting an entire human baby, then why are we astonished that God could manifest some feathers?

We serve a supernatural God, and we should therefore live an exciting supernatural life filled with experiences of God, the Holy Spirit and His angels. The supernatural does manifest into the natural. It always has, and it always will.

Birdmen

In our church, Pier49, in Rio, Brazil, we constantly encourage people to walk in an awareness of the presence of angels and to thank God for sending them. Recently, during one of our worship services, the two-year-old son of one of our leaders turned to his mother, pulled on her dress to get her attention and said, "Mommy, Mommy . . ."

"What is it, son?" his mother asked.

"Look, Mommy!" The little boy pointed up to the ceiling above the altar.

"What, baby? What are you seeing?" she asked, not knowing what he was pointing at.

"There, Mommy, there . . . see?" He pointed all around the ceiling.

"What is it? Mommy can't see it," she knelt down beside him and asked.

"Birdmen, Mommy, birdmen!" the little boy said with a big, happy smile.

"What are the birdmen doing, son?"

"They're flying." He immediately started to mimic what he saw, folding his little arms like wings and wiggling them all around. "They're flying like this." He ran in circles, flapping his cute little wings and shouting, "Birdmen, birdmen flying all around us!"

Not long after that, numerous feathers started to manifest, floating gently in the air and landing on the floor.

Do Angels Have Wings?

When we hear about feathers manifesting in our meetings, the first association people make is with angels. That is because for centuries pictures and illustrations have normally depicted angels as having wings. Movies and TV series such as *Touched by an Angel, Angels in America, Michael, Constantine, Legion* and so many others present the angels as winged creatures. But do angels really have wings?

In the Bible, most of the time the angels appear without any mention of wings. When the three angels appeared to Abraham in Genesis 18, he thought they were men. There is no mention of wings in that particular Scripture. When an angel appeared to Samson's parents, they just called him a "man of God" (see Judges 13:6–11). Once again, there is no mention of wings of any kind. Hebrews 13:2 (KJV) says that some people have "entertained angels unawares." If the people were unaware, that means they did not know that they were entertaining angels. If the angels had wings, the people entertaining them probably would have noticed they were angels, don't you think? When the church was praying for Peter and they were told he was at the gate, they thought it was his angel—indicating that the early Church expected angels to look like human beings, without wings. (For a comprehensive list of angelic manifestations with and without wings, refer to chapter 12.)

The earliest Christian image we know of that depicts an angel is located in the Catacomb of Priscilla on the Via Salaria, an ancient Roman road in Italy. This image, dated to the middle of the third century, depicts the annunciation of the virgin birth of Jesus and portrays the angel Gabriel without wings. Other representations of angels on sarcophagi and objects such as lamps and reliquaries of that same period also show angels without wings.[3] That strongly suggests that the angels who visited the apostles and their disciples in the early Church of the first century did not have wings.

Scripture never attributes wings to the angels who appear to humanity. Nevertheless, we know of at least two categories of angels who do have wings—the cherubim and seraphim (see Exodus 25:20; Isaiah 6; Ezekiel 10). In the Bible, these angelic beings are mentioned as being present on important occasions. The winged cherubim were sent to guard the Garden of Eden after Adam and Eve sinned. Cherubim and seraphim were seen in various visions that came to God's people, and they are representative figures in the Ark of the Covenant and in the Temple. The idea that some angelic creatures have wings is therefore also biblically valid. Daniel describes the angel in his vision as having a "swift flight" (Daniel 9:21). Though the prophet does not clearly mention the word *wings*, the passage leads us to believe that the angel he saw had them.

The Bible tells us, then, that some angels have wings and others do not. Whether these are permanent wings in permanent physical bodies or are mere anthropomorphisms (since the angels could have mass-free, ethereal bodies, as we discussed in chapter 9) is yet to be revealed to us.

Angelic Food

When we talk about feathers manifesting in our meetings, or anywhere for that matter, it is important to understand that we are talking about the materialization of the spiritual realm into our natural realm. An interesting passage in 1 Kings shows us such an event happening when an angel visits Elijah and gives him food:

> Then he [Elijah] lay down under the bush and fell asleep.
>
> All at once an angel touched him and said, "Get up and eat." He looked around, and there by his head was some bread baked over hot coals, and a jar of water. He ate and drank and then lay down again.
>
> 1 Kings 19:5–6

In this passage the angel brought the prophet bread and a jar of water. These elements were not in the spiritual realm, but in the natural. It was real bread, a real jar (probably of real clay) and real water. By saying *real*, I am not saying that things in the spirit are not real. I do believe that the true and everlasting reality is the spiritual one, for this physical reality will pass and the other will last forever. What I mean by *real* here is that something is tangible in such a way that the human senses can experience it. If an angel can bring bread and water, why not bring feathers or gold dust or precious gems? After all, according to the Bible, heaven is covered in gold and precious stones. If we believe that angels walk about on heavenly streets of gold, why is it so hard to believe that they would bring some gold dust from heaven on their feet?

Here is a second time that an angel brings Elijah food:

> The angel of the LORD came back a second time and touched him and said, "Get up and eat, for the journey is too much for you." So he got up and ate and drank. Strengthened by that food, he traveled forty days and forty nights until he reached Horeb, the mountain of God.
>
> 1 Kings 19:7–8

If an angel can manifest a meal to someone, why can't an angel manifest a feather?

Why would God do that kind of thing, manifesting a feather? you may wonder. First of all, because God is God and can do whatever He pleases, even if it is not in the Bible. Look at all the things Jesus did that had no former scriptural precedent: He walked on water, turned water into wine, healed a blind man with His spit and had Peter catch a specific fish that had a coin in its mouth. None of these cases had a biblical precedent before Jesus' time, yet God did them. The Torah made no biblical reference to any of these miracles Jesus performed, yet that did not prevent Jesus from doing them.

Second, because we have biblical precedent for angels manifesting natural objects. We just examined two texts where a spiritual being (an angel) gave a natural being (a man) something solid that was made of matter (a meal). There is our biblical precedent to affirm that angels can manifest solid objects into our world.

Still, we should not assume that all feathers that manifest in our midst are angel feathers. I have been in meetings in an old building where there were lots of pigeons and lots of feathers floating around, and the speaker announced from the platform that they were angel feathers. I went to that preacher later to exhort him that he was wrong and that those feathers were not a manifestation from God, but rather were pigeon feathers. He would not hear me out and continued to hype up the meetings by saying that God was doing things, when in reality they were not really happening. This preacher went on and on with this kind of behavior and refused to listen to exhortation, until he was deceived by demons and ended up preaching about UFOs, aliens and the like. His lack of humility ended up really hurting his ministry, and today many doors are closed to him.

We must be careful not to be too quick to announce a miracle or a manifestation, because we do not want to promote something God is *not doing*. On the other hand, we must be careful *not to undermine what God is doing*, either, lest we touch His glory. We must not prevent people from acknowledging His signs and wonders, and thus rob Him of praise for what He is indeed doing.

Are They Really Angel Feathers?

Feathers that show up in meetings are a reality all around the world. But we should not call them "angel feathers," because we don't know for sure that they come from angels. They could come from another heavenly being. The Bible contains an interesting account of a spiritual being—a rather important one, in fact—who has manifested feathers into this world. This being is even more important and more relevant to us than the angels.

Do you know whom I am talking about? No? It was the Holy Spirit Himself: "And the Holy Spirit descended on him in bodily form like a dove" (Luke 3:22). This passage shows that the Holy Spirit manifested on Jesus as a dove in the natural realm—not a spiritual dove, but a physical one *in bodily form*. Here is a strong biblical precedent for feathers manifesting from heaven, for the Holy Spirit did not manifest one or two feathers, but an entire dove covered in feathers.

Regarding feathers, I have read that a lot of skeptics say, "Angels are spiritual beings, and God makes His angels flames of fire. They are spiritual; they do not have wings or feathers." That is a misunderstanding of God's ways. We have already tackled the subject that God's angels manifest in the natural realm with physical bodies. The Bible shows us that angels can manifest with material bodies. Now we are talking about the Holy Spirit Himself coming up with some feathers as He turns into a dove—a real dove. A dove with real feathers! I wonder if some of these feathers fell in the meeting when the Holy Spirit flapped His real dove wings to fly up to Jesus' shoulders. The Bible does not say that it happened, but we can safely assume it did. After all, feathers fall from birds.

Take It to the FDA

Of course, there were skeptics in Moses' time and in Jesus' time, and there will be in our time as well. One skeptic, a researcher who believes he is spending his time wisely by trying to debunk the signs and wonders in the Word of Faith movement, got hold of some of these feathers that fell in a meeting and sent them to an ornithologist at the Science Advisory Board. In the ornithologist's responding statement dated November 12, 2008, the scientist wrote back, "The feathers you sent me are very obviously like normal bird feathers, and there is nothing about them to suggest they are other than bird."

This statement was enough to delight the skeptics, who affirmed, "See, these are just bird feathers."

I find that extremely interesting. Imagine if, in Jesus' time, there had been ornithologists and DNA testing and all the equipment necessary to study feathers and their origins. Imagine a Pharisee coming up close to Jesus and grabbing hold of a feather that had just fallen from the dove on Jesus' shoulder. Imagine with me that this Pharisee sends it off to the lab to have it analyzed by the ornithologists. What would they have found out? Let's take a look:

"Stop all this nonsense!" shouts the Pharisee, followed by his two friends. He is waving a piece of papyrus in the air as he approaches Jesus, who is breaking bread and having His disciples give it to a large group of people in the desert.

"See here?" the Pharisee continues, his long beard swaying in the wind. "This is the result of a test we have just received from the Galilean Birds of Prey Institute."

"That's right," says one of his Pharisee friends, nodding his head.

"You see," the first one says, turning to the multitude, who are curiously listening, "we picked up a feather from the alleged Holy Spirit . . ." (he does the quote sign with his fingers, quite theatrically), "who supposedly came in the bodily form of a dove . . ." (he does the quote sign again) "and who supposedly rested upon Jesus."

He pauses for a little while, as if waiting for someone to say something. Instead, the people go back to quietly minding their own business and sharing the bread and fish the disciples are handing them.

"The results have arrived!" the Pharisee announces through his thick beard.

"Yes, the results have arrived," his two friends echo.

"And guess what it says, Jesus. Huh?" the Pharisee demands. Jesus carries on without responding to the man.

"Well," the Pharisee shouts toward the crowd, "the ornithologist sent this document about that feather I got from the alleged manifestation of the supposed Holy Spirit that rested upon You in the bodily form of a dove, good Rabbi. . . ." The Pharisee elbows his friends, with a crooked smile. "And I quote: 'The feathers you sent me are obviously like normal bird feathers, and there is nothing about them to suggest they are other than bird!'"

He shouts the second half of the statement out loud for the crowd. Then he looks around to see if anyone is sympathizing with his phenomenal discovery. "Don't you see that this man is a fraud?" he shouts to the multitude.

"Brother Jacob!" One of his friends pulls urgently on his garment.

The Pharisee just keeps shouting, "It was no Holy Spirit resting upon Jesus; it was just a dove!"

"Brother Jacob, please!" His friend pulls the sleeve of his robe again, harder this time.

But Brother Jacob is too excited about his recent discovery. "Just wait a minute, Brother Eli. This is an official document from the Galilean Birds of Prey Institute, and it clearly says that the bird that rested upon Him was just a dove—nothing more than a casual, regular, ordinary bird! This is scientific proof that it was not the Holy Spirit! Had it been the Holy Spirit, the results would have said the feathers were not from this world."

"I'm sorry, Brother Jacob," Eli insists, "but I don't think these people are interested in what you're saying." Brother Esau nods frantically in agreement.

"And why is that, brothers?" Jacob asks.

"Well, we just saw Jesus' disciples take five little loaves of bread and two little fish, and look . . ." They point to the multitude sitting on the ground, eating. "They fed all these people! At least five thousand men . . ."

"And not only that," says Brother Esau, "but the disciples have gathered twelve baskets full of bread and fish left over."

"So?" says Jacob, the papyrus document still in his hand.

"Don't you think it's a miracle?" asks Eli.

Brother Jacob looks around at the multitude of people sitting on the ground, their hunger fully satisfied with the feast Jesus is providing. He looks over his shoulders, leans closer to his Pharisee brothers and whispers, "Brother Eli, you and Brother Esau go down and pretend you're part of the multitude. Pick up some samples of bread and fish, and then we'll see what the FDA in Jerusalem has to say about it. . . ."

In conclusion, don't waste your time and energy trying to make a convert out of a skeptic. Jesus Himself, despite all the miracles He performed, could not do so. Leave them to God and to the Holy Spirit. They know exactly how and when to change a Saul into a Paul.

The feathers on the wings of the Holy Spirit were real feathers, of course, because God had decided that the Holy Spirit would come rest upon Jesus in the bodily form of a dove as a sign of the Spirit's infilling and indwelling. This is very different from what we discussed in chapter 9 about the bodies of angels. It is a clear scriptural account of the Holy Spirit's materialization *in bodily form*. It does not say that the Spirit was a bird of light or a bird of fire, but a *real* dove, just as when the angels brought *real* food to Elijah, and later also to Jesus. If there had been Pharisees who wanted to do a DNA test on the food the angels "allegedly" brought, guess what? The DNA test would have shown them that it was real food, not heavenly food. My point being, the Bible shows us that God does materialize things, be it feathers or food, from the heavenly realm into the natural realm.

Of Course God Can!

The Holy Spirit manifested in the form of a real dove that had real feathers. What if God wants to do it again and manifests feathers in a meeting as a sign of the Holy Spirit's presence and manifestation? And what if these feathers are nothing but real feathers? Can God manifest real bird feathers to His servants? Of course He can. He manifested real food from angels; He manifested real water from a rock; the Holy Spirit manifested as a real bird.

Again, you may be wondering, *Why would God do something like that? What's the purpose?* If you can figure out why Jesus walked on water or why He ascended into heaven before the apostles' eyes, maybe you also will be able to figure out why God would manifest feathers, gold dust and precious gems in meetings.

The Kingdom of God is a Kingdom of mystery. There is so much mystery involving God. "The secret things belong to the LORD our God" (Deuteronomy 29:29). Have you figured out how the Trinity works, or do you just accept it by faith? Have you simply accepted that there is a supernatural element involved in communion's bread and wine, or do you want to send samples to the FDA for testing after these elements have been blessed?

It is about time that we open our hearts as little children and just believe. Believe in the supernatural, believe in angels, believe in feathers, believe in gold dust, believe in gems from heaven—believe in whatever God does when you cry out for Him to come manifest His presence. And don't wait until you see it to believe it, either. Believe by faith, for as Jesus said in John 20:29, "Blessed are those who have not seen and yet have believed."

12

Signs That Make You Wonder

> I persevered in demonstrating among you the marks of a true apostle, including signs, wonders and miracles.
>
> 2 Corinthians 12:12

Most of God's supernatural acts recorded in Scripture had no biblical precedent until they happened. In fact, most of them were never repeated again, either. Nobody had ever made an ax head float until Elisha did it (see 2 Kings 6:1–7). There was no scriptural background for it, but that did not prevent Elisha from performing this miracle.

A lot of people ask, "Why would God make feathers, gold dust or gemstones appear?" Well, why did God make Moses' staff turn into a serpent? Why did He make Aaron's staff blossom? Why did He make fire fall from heaven when Elijah prayed? Why did He make the ax head float when Elisha prayed? None of these people had any biblical precedent to fall back on when they took part in these signs.

So why did God do such things? How did the people who saw them happen know it was really God? Why didn't they stone Moses or Aaron or Elijah or Elisha as sorcerers? Because God had called these men and sent them as representatives to His people. By performing such signs through them, God was bringing glory to His name.

It Is All by Faith

We are living in a tremendous time, a time when God again is allowing men to interact empirically with His supernatural realm. He is opening the gates of heaven and literally showering people with His grace through heavenly signs, wonders, visitations and angelic encounters that forever will change those who experience them. These supernatural experiences have branded the core of the relationship between God and men throughout history, particularly men to whom and through whom God first manifested Himself.

Think about it: God revealed Himself to Noah in what way? By prophetically revealing His plans to destroy the earth and simultaneously showing Noah how to save his entire family and consequently mankind through building an ark. I believe angels and other supernatural manifestations were present during that whole process.

People in Noah's time not only did not have a biblical precedent for what they were seeing; they did not have a Bible or even the Torah to go to so they could check to see if what Noah was claiming was true. How could they know for sure that what this crazy old man was saying about a flood coming was accurate?

Likewise, can we know for sure that manifestations such as feathers, gold dust and precious gems are from God? Can we prove they are from heaven? "Faith is confidence in what we hope for and assurance about what we do not see" (Hebrews 11:1). It is all by faith. Let me ask you one thing, and if you can answer it, I will answer you about these signs: Can we know for sure that God exists? Can we prove that He is in heaven?

Whom Does God Use?

Of course, there are those who will ask, "That's fine that God manifested Himself to holy people in the Bible, but who are we to think He will perform signs through regular folks like us?"

That question shows a lack of understanding about God's nature and selective process. None of the people He used in the Bible were fit to be used, "for all have sinned and fall short of the glory of God" (Romans 3:23). As Henry Blackaby, the author of *Experiencing God*, said, "The reality is that the Lord never calls the qualified; He qualifies the called." Let's take a look at a few of the people God called and used for His glory:

- Noah was a drunk (see Genesis 9:20–21).
- Abraham was a liar (see Genesis 12:10–13; 20:1–2).
- Jacob was a liar and a deceiver (see Genesis 27:19).
- Moses was an assassin (see Exodus 2:11–14).
- Samson was a womanizer and a fornicator (see Judges 16:1).
- Rahab was a prostitute (see Joshua 2:1).
- David was an adulterer and a murderer (see 2 Samuel 11:1–27).

And that is only in the Old Testament. What should we say about Jesus' disciples? Peter had a problem with his temper. Thomas had no faith. Judas betrayed Jesus. (A lot of people tend to discount Judas, but they forget that he was part of Jesus' ministry and served Him for almost four years.) No, God does not manifest heaven through us based on who we are, but rather, based on who He is.

There is one factor, however, that does distinguish those who have an encounter with God from those who do not: *hunger*. God said that those who seek shall find. I believe the opposite is also true. If you are not seeking God's supernatural signs, they will not manifest in your life and ministry. Further, you probably will not recognize signs as coming from God when you see them happening in other people's lives and ministries.

I am convinced that hunger for more of God is the sorting factor between those who experience supernatural encounters and manifestations and those who do not. After all, Jesus used to ask people, "What do you want me to do for you?" (Matthew 20:32; Mark 10:36, 51; Luke 18:41). Many times, Jesus told someone that the outcome the person saw was the result of his or her faith. He said as much to the centurion about his son's healing, to the paralytic in Nazareth, to the woman with the issue of blood and to many others (see Matthew 8:5–13; 9:2–8, 20–22; Mark 5:25–34; Luke 5:17–26; 8:43–48). We hear it from Jesus Himself that it will be done according to our faith. If you have faith, if you believe something, if you want it and expect it to happen, it will be so to you. If not—if you think this is not of God and you do not expect it—guess what . . . ?

Without faith we cannot please God. He has made heaven available for us and has invited us to taste it. He does not force it, nor does He impose it on us. It is our job to answer the invitation to dig deeper into His supernatural realm, the realm that Jesus literally—in this world and in heaven—has unveiled for us.

Burning Bushes

One of my most powerful supernatural encounters happened in a season when I was more desperate for more of God than ever before in my life. This time there was a biblical precedent for what happened; it was in the story of Moses and the burning bush. It was a glorious encounter that I experienced with some friends on a mountaintop where we would usually go to pray. I believe it happened because we were so hungry for more of God. It was a little after 3:00 a.m., and we had been there worshiping and praying since 8:00 p.m. the previous night. Even though we had been praying for seven straight hours, nobody felt sleepy. Rather, we were all burning up with passion for Jesus. We were speaking in tongues and singing songs of worship, with tears running from our eyes, as this intense passion for God burned within our hearts. Suddenly, all around us, several bushes started glowing with an intense lemon-yellow color, much like glow sticks. I was on my knees, praying with my forehead touching the dirt. Every now and then I would take a peek at the glowing twigs around us and laugh for joy.

I remember praying, *O Lord, let me see Your angels.* A few minutes went by, and then I felt this swift touch of cloth rubbing against my left arm. I peeked and saw feet wearing sandals under a white robe. I looked up and there they were, three angels, walking among us in the middle of the glowing bushes. When I saw them, an uncontrollable fear took over my entire body, and I began to shake involuntarily.

I prayed, *Father, give me Your peace, please . . . give me Your peace.* The trembling went away, and a tremendous peace came upon me. I looked around and saw all those bushes glowing brightly in the dark, and I immediately understood what the Bible meant when it said, "There the angel of the LORD appeared to him in flames of fire from within a bush. Moses saw that though the bush was on fire it did not burn up" (Exodus 3:2).

We stayed there and prayed and cried and laughed in the presence of God and His holy angels all night, until the sun came up. The result of that encounter was even more hunger for God. Seeing the angels and the burning bushes was a fantastic experience, but it would have been an empty experience if it were not for the manifest presence of God we felt in that place. Encounters like this only increased my passion and desire for Him as I continued my journey into my calling and destiny. To this day, my cry is, and always will be, "More, Lord! I want You more, and I want more of You!"

Gold Dust

Our church family is so aware of angelic presences that it is commonplace for them to see signs and supernatural manifestations not only during our services but anytime, anywhere. One of the most common signs that happen wherever we are is gold dust. It is normal for our church people to have gold dust manifest when they are sharing their faith with unbelievers. Many people have come to the Lord after witnessing this sign.

One day a young man from our church was at the barbershop getting a haircut, when all of a sudden he noticed his hands got covered with glittery, shimmering gold dust.

His barber asked, "What's that? Are you playing with glitter glue?"

"Oh, no," the young man replied. "This is not glitter glue. . . ."

"Okay." The barber shook his head. "What is it, then?"

"Gold dust," the young man answered.

"Gold dust?" The barber squeezed one eye and raised the opposite brow.

"Yeah. Sometimes it falls from the angels," the young man said with a smile.

"Gold dust from the angels? How come?" the barber asked, wrinkling his forehead.

"Angelic manifestations are common in our church, and sometimes it happens wherever we go," the young man told the barber with a smile.

"But why would God do something like that?" the barber asked.

"That's a common question," the young man replied. "Have you ever heard that there are streets of gold in heaven?"

"Yes, I suppose," the barber answered.

At this point the clients sitting in other chairs, as well as two other barbers, got interested in the conversation. They all were listening now.

"And do you believe in guardian angels?" the young man asked.

"I guess," his barber replied, shrugging his shoulders.

A couple of the other clients muttered "yeah" as well, nodding to each other.

"You see," the young man continued, "my pastor says that our guardian angels always carry some gold dust from the streets of heaven on their feet when they come to watch over us."

The barbers and the other clients all looked at each other and nodded positively.

"That's very interesting," said the young man's barber. "Tell us more about the angels."

The conversation that followed led to a discussion about the Gospel. By the time his haircut was done, that young man had led the barbers and the other clients in the barbershop to the Lord.

If one soul will repent and come into the Kingdom because that person saw a feather or a gold flake or a precious stone manifest in our midst as we worship, then that is enough reason for us to join the angels and rejoice over these signs. I want to invite you to open your heart and have childlike faith. Celebrate God for the "birdmen," the feathers, the gold dust, the precious stones or whatever He decides to do to bring glory to His holy and precious name. God is sovereign. He can do all things.

Gold Teeth

Let me tell you about my favorite manifestation, which I have not mentioned yet. It is gold teeth. I love to know that God is concerned about us even to the point of caring about small details such as our dental fillings. I have seen two kinds of gold teeth. The first kind is when God changes mercury-based metal fillings into gold. The second kind is when a decayed tooth itself changes into gold. In other words, the process can be partial or complete. Partial is when only a small filling turns into gold; complete is when an entire tooth turns into gold. Both are common in our revival meetings in Brazil, and both show a loving Father's care for His children.

I remember one night when Randy Clark had me give words of knowledge at our yearly conference called Voice of the Apostles, or VOA. This one took place in Orlando, Florida, and there were at least six thousand people in that particular meeting. I remember that I pointed out to the crowd and gave many words of knowledge. That night I prayed for many people, and they got healed of several conditions. I specifically recall calling out deaf ears. I did not have a word of knowledge for deaf ears, but Father God has given me the gift of faith for the healing of the deaf. That night, sixteen people stood up for healing of deaf ears. I prayed for them, and they all signaled that they were hearing again. There was a lot of joy and laughter as they celebrated their healing with their friends and loved ones.

As I stood there on that tall stage overlooking the crowd, suddenly the taste of metal filled my mouth. *What is this, my Love?* I asked the Holy Spirit. (Many years ago I had a profound experience with the Holy Spirit in which I felt totally and utterly embraced by His overwhelming love. Since that day, I have been calling Him *my Love*.)

Gold teeth, He answered me.

I turned to the multitude and announced over the microphone, "God is giving someone here gold teeth. It could be more than one person." I pointed out toward the crowd again. "You'll know if it is you because you'll have a sudden taste of metal in your mouth. If that's you, ask someone you know to look inside your mouth and check if you've gotten a gold tooth. If you have, wave both hands over your head so we can see what God is doing and glorify His name."

I could see a little commotion where some people were laughing and jumping around one guy and then another. The guys looked at me, smiling with their mouths open and pointing inside.

"Did you get a gold tooth?" I asked them.

They nodded.

"Well, wave your hands over your head to testify."

They did. They waved their hands over their head to testify that they had received gold teeth. Later that night, another lady contacted me to tell me she had also gotten a gold tooth.

This is also common in Brazil. Wherever we preach, we give God the chance to manifest His love and power by giving people gold teeth, and He does so. We have hundreds of pictures and videos of people who have gotten gold teeth. In my congregation, many people have received three or four gold teeth. Some have even had up to seven fillings turn into gold. Some of them have had entire crowns turn into gold. My mother-in-law received a big gold crown, and one of my leaders received four.

This happens not only in Brazil, but also in many other countries where people cannot afford dental work and end up with tooth decay. It is common in revival meetings all over the world—especially in places where people cannot afford dental treatment—to see Father God change bad, rotten teeth into whole teeth with brand-new gold crowns.

Why would God change amalgam fillings into gold? you may wonder. Amalgam is an archaic filling material that is made of between 43 percent and 54 percent mercury. Many studies have shown that it is unstable after it is manipulated and implanted into human teeth, where it constantly releases highly toxic mercury vapor. The mercury is a neurotoxin, yet many dentists are implanting such amalgam fillings an inch from their patients' brains. Also, implanting an amalgam filling requires the removal of a significant amount of healthy tooth matter, and this weakens overall tooth structure and health. As if all that were not enough, amalgam fillings expand and contract over time due to temperature changes in the mouth, causing teeth to crack and creating the need for more dental work. So when the presence of God manifests in a meeting where people have amalgam fillings, it is common to see those fillings turn into gold. Why gold? Gold is a superior metal that does not carry mercury or any other toxin. Gold fillings don't break or fracture, they expand similar to tooth structure, they don't absorb oral fluids, and they don't change shape.[1]

As we gather together in God's holy name and cry out to Him for healing, Father God walks into the building and sees many of His children who have dangerous amalgam fillings in their teeth. What would an almighty, loving Father do? That's right—He would change these fillings into gold, and time after time He does it.

Gold Hair

Besides gold dust and gold teeth, there have even been instances of gold hair. Once when I preached in a church in Alaska, gold dust and gold hair manifested on people's heads. After the service I went to my friend's house, and we were all talking about the meeting and how God had shown up. The people at my friend's told me it was not the first time that signs like that had happened in their meetings. I told them I had seen gold dust before, but not gold hair.

We had brought a gold hair with us from the service, formerly a long, blond hair from one of the ladies who had been in the church. I started investigating the strand of hair because it fascinated me. It amazed me that the hair looked half normal, and then it looked as though it simply became a fine gold ribbon. I sighed as I looked at it and said, "I wish we had a microscope to check out how it meshes. I mean, what does it look like where the hair becomes gold?"

"I have one!" my friend said, getting up and rushing to the back of the house. In less than a minute he showed up again with a smile. "Here," he said as he handed me a microscope.

"Awesome!" I said, taking it from him and setting it on the table. I placed the hair that had turned into gold under the microscope and carefully analyzed it. "It's hair, all right," I said. "You can see all the scales of the hair fibers, just as you see in shampoo commercials." Then, as my eyes kept moving down the length of the hair, I exclaimed, "Wait a minute! This hair turns into a fine, perfectly flat gold ribbon right in the middle of its length!" It amazed me to see how it suddenly became gold.

People ask me, "Why would God do these things?" It is so simple; it is nothing more than a loving Father blessing His children and caring for their needs.

Gems from Heaven

Gemstones from heaven are another wonderful sign that is becoming more and more commonplace around the world. It is common for gems to appear around people when I am leading worship or praying for healing. Not long ago I was ministering at a church in Sao Paulo, Brazil, and precious stones started to manifest around me and around the people I was praying for. Many people were healed that night, including a young man and a young woman who each had one leg three inches shorter than their other one.

A couple of weeks ago I was preaching in our church, Pier49, in Rio, Brazil. I had just shared with the church about how much Jesus loves us, and I added that Jesus sometimes sends gifts of precious gems and gold to us today as a reminder that we are His Bride and that our celestial wedding is soon to come. I then asked the worship team to play, and I told the church to worship our King, our Bridegroom, and to declare our love for Him.

A few minutes went by as we stood there in worship. His thick presence filled the air; it was so precious and tangible. It did not take long for precious stones and gold specks to start manifesting all around us. I told people to expect it to happen and to keep an eye open to see manifestations such as these gems, gold dust and feathers. As people started to look around with expectation, many signs did take place. (Signs and wonders only happen when we expect them. Today, Jesus is still saying, "Let it be according to your faith.") Diamonds, emeralds, amethysts and gold specks started to fall from heaven all around us as we stood there in worship.

Somebody brought us a little velvet jewelry box, and we placed all the gems in it as they kept coming—beautiful gems of all colors, shapes and sizes. More and more people started coming up to the stage to bring gems of different and brilliant colors. There were also little specks of gold, along with some quite big flakes. We all praised Jesus for blessing us with His presence and for adorning us, His Bride, for our upcoming wedding. The supernatural realm manifested in the natural in a wonderful way that amazed and blessed everyone. (Often, these manifestations disappear later in the same way that they appeared, but not always. Sometimes some gold flakes will remain, and we usually place them in a little box, together with the gems.)

At the end of the service, a beloved sister came to me and said, "Ed, do you see that lady on the floor?"

I looked down and saw this young lady crying and laughing, which is a fairly normal thing to see happening at Pier49.

"Yes," I said, "I see her."

"That's a friend of mine," she continued, smiling. "She is—or I should say she was—an atheist. I've been trying to bring her to church for a long time, and she wouldn't come. For some reason she decided to come to this service, of all nights! If I had known this would happen, I wouldn't have brought her, because I know how skeptical she is—was."

I looked again and pointed at the lady laughing and crying on the floor. "Are you sure you're talking about her?" I asked with a smile.

"Yes," she laughed, "that's her right there."

"Wow!" I raised my brows. "What happened?"

Trying to control her laughter, she told me, "My friend was sitting there, and I could hear her saying, 'I don't believe this; I don't believe this.' She kept repeating it, like a mantra. Then, when you talked about the gold and gems, she opened her hand and looked up, as if trying to see if it were raining. All of a sudden, this huge gold flake manifested right in the middle of her palm. She started to say, 'I believe it, God; I believe it.' The Holy Spirit fell upon her, and she was sovereignly saved and baptized in the Holy Spirit. Now she is on the floor, crying, laughing and speaking in tongues."

An atheist was saved because she saw a sign. That would be reason enough for God to perform signs like these, don't you think? A lot of times people ask, "Why would God manifest feathers or gold dust in a meeting?" Here is your answer—as a sign of His supernatural presence not only to His children, but also to those who are lost. If it will take a gold flake manifesting in one of His lost daughter's hands to get her to open her heart to Him, you can bet your mustache He is going to make one appear for her. He does not want anyone to perish; He wants all to come to repentance (see 2 Peter 3:9).

Tares among the Wheat

A pastor friend of mine who has had the same signs happen at his church took some of these gemstones from a meeting to a geologist friend to have them analyzed. He said the geologist gave them back in two separate bags with labels that said *Real* and *Fake*. He told us the geologist said that some of the gems were real and others were not.

"I was not surprised at all by that," my friend told me. "I could tell myself that some of the gems the people in the congregation brought forward were not real. They looked more like something that had fallen off a dress or a lady's sandal."

As I thought about what my friend had told me, it occurred to me that when people walk around looking down on the floor for precious gems from heaven, they also will find all sorts of other shiny things that look like precious stones but are not real ones. When you seek the real, you have to be prepared for the fake.

There is no way you can make room for supernatural signs from God and not have some fake or mistaken things come along with them. Some people do it by mistake and others do it on purpose, out of their orphan heart. Their need for people to notice them makes them do many things to call attention to themselves. I believe the truth eventually exposes people like that. But if we do not make room for dealing with the false, we will never have the real. That is why Jesus allowed the tares to grow among the wheat.

Real Gems

My friend went on to tell me that the geologist was amazed at the quality of the real stones. This geologist said that although the specific gravity of the stones he was testing did not match any stones he had ever seen in nature, they were real gemstones—not synthetic ones like cubic zirconia.

The geologist also said that the clarity of the stones was unique. All the real gems he tested were translucent, with fine color, except for the colorless diamonds. Their hardness did not match any stones he had ever seen or studied. In the natural, the hardness (scratch resistance) of precious gems ranges from 1 to 10. The opal family, for example, ranges around 5–6, while the emerald family ranges around 7–8. Diamonds measure 10 on the hardness scale, which is why tiny diamonds are used in glass-cutting tools. According to the geologist, however, all the real gems that my friend had given him for testing measured above 11 in their hardness, which made no sense to him. Other technical and geological specifications in the heaven-sent gems did not match that of regular precious stones on the market, either.

Out of curiosity, my friend asked the geologist about the price range of the stones he brought in for testing. The geologist replied that since there was no documentation associating them to any certified manufacturer or any way of tracing them back to their original source, there would be no way anyone could put a price tag on them. My friend was not a bit disappointed to hear that. In fact, he was excited because he had never thought of selling the stones. They were gifts from Jesus to His Bride.

I agree. I think these gems, which increasingly are appearing in churches all over the world, are a gift from Jesus to His Bride. They are a prophetic sign of the Second Coming of the Lord, our Bridegroom.

I heard something like the voice of a great multitude, and like the voice of many waters, and like the voice of mighty thunders, saying, "Hallelujah! For the Lord our God, the Almighty, reigns! Let us rejoice and be exceedingly glad, and let us give the glory to him. For the marriage of the Lamb has come, and his wife has made herself ready." It was given to her that she would array herself in bright, pure, fine linen: for the fine linen is the righteous acts of the saints.

He said to me, "Write, 'Blessed are those who are invited to the marriage supper of the Lamb.'"

Revelation 19:6–9 WEB

The King's Dowry

But what do gemstones have to do with the Second Coming? you may wonder. In biblical times, when the bride's parents gave their daughter in marriage, the social and cultural understanding was that they should receive adequate compensation for letting go of their girl. This compensation was the marriage dowry. It was not always required that the dowry be paid in cash; it could be paid in services.[2] For example, Jacob offered himself as a slave worker to Laban, saying, "I will serve you seven years for Rachel" (Genesis 29:18 WEB). Then Laban deceived Jacob by giving him Leah for a wife, so he ended up having to work another seven years to pay the dowry for Rachel. Another great dowry paid for a bride in the Bible was when Othniel gave an entire city as payment for Achsah, Caleb's daughter (see Judges 1:11–15).

Dowries were common not only in biblical times; the custom has been part of civil law in almost all countries, Europe included. Dowries also were important components in ancient Greek and Roman marriages. Failure to provide a dowry could cancel a marriage. It was customary for a king to give his fiancée's parents a dowry of precious stones and gold. William Shakespeare made use of this in *King Lear*. One of Cordelia's wooers ceases to woo her when he hears that King Lear will give her no dowry. Dowries are still expected and demanded as a condition for accepting a marriage proposal in many European countries, as well as in Northern Africa, the Balkans, South Asia, India, Africa and other parts of the world.[3]

For millennia now, Jesus' Bride, the Church, together with the Holy Spirit, has being crying out for the return of the Bridegroom. "The Spirit and the bride say, 'Come!'" (Revelation 22:17). I believe our Lord Jesus is finally getting ready to hear the cry of the Holy Spirit and His Bride. By His Bride, I don't only mean the Christians alive on the earth today, but also the thousands, and perhaps millions, of God's children who are already in heaven, patiently waiting for His glorious return and the establishment of His Kingdom forever. I am convinced that we are getting closer and closer to the end times, and our Lord is getting ready for His return. He is making preparations in heaven, summoning His hosts of angels and adorning His Bride with a dowry of precious gemstones to prepare her for that wonderful day.

Faith Is the Fruit

God can do all things. If He wants to manifest His glory through signs such as feathers, gold dust and gemstones, who are we to tell Him otherwise? As we have already seen, we cannot limit what God can do based on what He has done before. He always does new things. Nor can we decide if something is from God based on a biblical precedent. Many of the miracles He performed throughout the Bible were unique, never having occurred again, before or after. The same can be true today. If we were to use that measurement of a biblical precedent to judge whether Christ Jesus was from God, we would not believe in Him, because He performed many unprecedented signs and wonders. Walking on water was one; healing the sick with His spit was another. There was nothing in the Law to back those up, but Jesus did them anyway. Jesus showed us that biblical precedent is not a means of measuring whether or not a sign is from God. He also taught us the rule of thumb for knowing whether something is from God: "By their fruit you will recognize them" (Matthew 7:20).

What is the fruit of seeing angels or feathers or gold dust or gold teeth or precious gemstones from heaven? Faith. Faith is the unquestionable fruit that follows a supernatural manifestation, an encounter or a vision of this sort. Supernatural manifestations in someone's life often bring that person an exponential increase in faith. Having a supernatural experience such as seeing an angel or getting something from an angel will immediately skyrocket your faith.

God is creative. In fact, He invented creativity. He is always coming up with something new. In the case of manifestations, how do we know if something outside of biblical precedent is from God? That is a good question. Jonathan Edwards, the great revivalist preacher and theologian of the early eighteenth century, provided us with five "tests" to determine if a manifestation is a genuine work of God:

1. Does it honor the person of Jesus Christ?
2. Does it operate against the kingdom of darkness?
3. Does it produce a greater regard for Scripture?
4. Does it lead people into truth and light?
5. Does it produce a greater love for God and man?[4]

For ten years, I have been experiencing these unusual signs countless times in several countries around the world. As a senior pastor, I also have been able to follow up in the lives of many people in my church who have experienced and who still experience these things. When I consider Edwards's tests, I can safely say yes about these things to all five of his questions.

Open your heart, mind and spirit to receive revelation of God's truth. Our God is the same yesterday, today and forever. We cannot put God in a box. No box is large enough to contain Him, not even a biblical box. John himself said that all the books in the world would not be enough to describe all that Jesus said and did (see John 21:25). So open the box of your heart and the box of your mind to know and believe that God can do all things, even things that have no precedent in the Bible. He did such miracles, signs and wonders before, and He can do them again. As Randy Clark says, "The number one way in which God brings glory to His name in the Scriptures is through signs and wonders."

13

Angels in Your Life

Sometimes talking about angels raises as many questions as it answers. We have talked about them throughout this whole book—how they intervene in human history, how they act as our guardians and bring healing, when they come in worship and in prayer, the gifts and messages they can bring, what their "bodies" are composed of, what they look like and why we can or cannot see them. But for all of that information, there is still a lot we don't yet know about angels, and do you know what? That is okay. We don't know everything there is to know about angels—or about anything else in the Kingdom—and it is okay not to know! It is okay for some mystery to remain part of our faith. We don't have to know everything, do we? Some people think we do, but God thinks we don't. He often gives us information on a need-to-know basis, and there are a lot of things we don't need to know.

Are you comfortable with that? Jesus was. Did you ever notice how often He answered people's questions without giving them an answer? I love it when Jesus answers people's questions without actually answering them. I think it is fantastic. Think about the time that the disciples came to Him and asked about a blind man, "Rabbi, who sinned, this man or his parents, that he was born blind?" Jesus comes up with this wonderful answer: "Neither this man nor his parents sinned, but this happened so that the works of God might be displayed in him" (John 9:3). And off Jesus goes to heal the man by spitting on the ground, making some mud with the saliva and putting it on the man's eyes. He tells him to go wash in the Pool of Siloam, which the man does, and he goes home seeing. The disciples marvel at the miracle and end up forgetting their original question about who was at fault for the blindness. I think that after seeing someone blind from birth healed in such a way, with such authority, most of us would forget our questions as well.

Sometimes God's perspective on what is important is very different from ours. We tend to think we need to know how everything works. We have this urge to get information about all the whys. Especially today, living in the "Information Age," we feel as though we need to know all the inner workings of the Kingdom. But do you know what? We cannot really understand it all, and God is not really concerned about fully explaining Himself. I don't see Jesus a bit concerned about explaining how He did things—how He turned water into wine or how He raised the dead. He did not even leave us with a detailed manual on how to raise the dead or how to heal the sick, yet He told us to do both. We need to trust that God will reveal to us what we need to know.

Speaking of leaving us an instruction manual, do you know why Jesus did not write any gospels for us Himself, as the apostles did? It is because He left us something much better. He sent us the Author of all Scripture, the Holy Spirit, to live inside us. Let the Holy Spirit of God, who dwells inside you, guide you into what you need to know: "But when he, the Spirit of truth, comes, he will guide you into all the truth" (John 16:13).

All that said, it is still interesting to talk about all the things we know—and don't know—about angels. In this final chapter, let's take one more look at what we know about them. We will look at some facts, some interesting speculations by different theologians and some angelic job descriptions right from the pages of Scripture. Taken all together, they give us a good picture of who the angels are, what they do and how you and I might expect that they will intervene in our lives. What a wonderful gift our heavenly Father has given us in all the ways that these important angelic beings interact with us, His children.

Five Important and Curious Facts about Angels

We do know a few things for certain about angels. These are facts borne out by Scripture, even though people often believe a lot of myths and traditions that go against them, especially when it comes to the first two. Here are five important and curious facts we know for sure about angels:

1. Angels are not humans who have died. Some movies and TV shows have popularized the idea that when people die, they go to heaven and get their wings. But that is not how it works. Scripture says, "It is appointed unto men once to die, but after this the judgment" (Hebrews 9:27 KJV). People don't become angels, and angels are not people who have died.

2. There are no baby angels in the Bible. Again, popular culture has given people a false impression about angels, picturing them as tiny baby cherubs floating around valentine hearts and flowers. But no angels I have ever seen had anything either tiny or babyish about them. They are majestic and powerful beings that elicit fear from humans as our natural first response, not cries of "How cute!"

3. Angels can disguise themselves as everyday people. In an earlier chapter we looked at some instances where people were in the presence of angels and did not realize it because the angels appeared human. Hebrews 13:2 (NKJV) tells us this can happen: "Do not forget to entertain strangers, for by so doing some have unwittingly entertained angels." That alone gives us a good reason to show hospitality to others.

4. *Angels have names and personalities.* The Bible gives us the names of two good angels, Gabriel and Michael, who play important roles in human history. While it does not give us the name of every angel it mentions, the fact that these angels have names suggests that God probably named all the angels.

5. *Angels are asexual beings.* Although human art has long depicted angels as either large, armor-clad males with swords or flowery females with long golden hair and flowing robes, the reality is neither. Matthew 22:30 gives us reason to believe they are asexual: "At the resurrection people will neither marry nor be given in marriage; they will be like the angels in heaven."

An Angelic Hierarchy

Along with the scriptural information we know about the angels, prominent theologians have put forth some speculations that seem very plausible about the hierarchy of angels. The most influential model of an angelic hierarchy was put forward by Pseudo-Dionysius the Areopagite in the fifth century in his book *De Coelesti Hierarchia* (*On the Celestial Hierarchy*). Thomas Aquinas later built on this same model in the thirteenth century in his best-known work, the *Summa Theologica*. Both writers based their texts on passages from the New Testament, particularly Ephesians 1:21 and Colossians 1:16, to develop three hierarchies, spheres or triads of angels, with each containing three orders or choirs.

Pseudo-Dionysius and Aquinas both drew on the New Testament, yet the biblical canon is relatively silent on the subject.

As a result, we view their hierarchy models as highly speculative. Yet they very well could be accurate, so let's take a closer look at them.[1]

- First Sphere—these angels are the heavenly servants of God; they typically are in His presence around His throne.
  - Seraphim
  - Cherubim
  - Thrones

- Second Sphere—these angels work as the governors of creation; they guide and rule angelic activity and make war on evil spirits.
  - Dominions or Lordships
  - Virtues or Strongholds
  - Powers or Authorities

- Third Sphere—these angels function as guides, protectors and messengers to mankind; they have the most interaction with people and include the guardian angels.
  - Principalities or Rulers
  - Archangels
  - Angels

An Angelic Job Description

So many different sources say so many different things about angels that I thought it would be useful to talk about what it is that angels really do—what their "job description" is, according to the Bible.

It is important for us to understand that the angels are under God's command, not ours—at least not during this period of our existence, while we see only a reflection, as if through a mirror (see 1 Corinthians 13:12). Later, as we receive full revelation of our sonship in heaven, we will be higher than the angels (see 1 Corinthians 6:3). During the human, carnal and temporal period of our existence, however, the angels do not submit to our orders and commands. There are no biblical precedents for people commanding the angels. It is our Father in heaven who commands them to come and serve us. Even Jesus, when He referred to having angels help and protect Him, did not say He Himself would call upon or give orders to them. Rather, He said He could ask the Father, and the Father would send His angels (see Matthew 26:53).

All the angels' activities take place in response to God's direction. Nevertheless, most of what the Bible reveals about what the angels do is related to us as humans. They protect us, serve us, feed us, surround us, bring messages to us from our Father, and much more. In this sense, one could say that angels are invisible spiritual supernannies of a sort, watching over and caring for the needs of their Master's children. I hope you find the following list useful as a detailed job description of what the angels do. To facilitate the search for certain passages about angels, I have sorted them into different subjects for you.

1. Angels worship God.

I think it is pretty much common knowledge that angels worship God. Who can stand before the Almighty One and not bow down in worship, right? I don't think it is possible. But they don't worship God because they have to; rather, they choose to. Worshiping God is not their primary job, but it is something the angels do as a natural consequence of contemplating His unfathomable glory.

Nehemiah 9:6

Job 38:7

Psalm 103:20; 148:2

Isaiah 6:1–6

Luke 2:8–14

Hebrews 1:6

Revelation 4:6–9; 5:11–14; 7:11–12; 14:3; 19:5–7; 22:8–9

2. Angels are sent to deliver messages.

Messengers—that is the angels' primary role in the Scriptures. They bring messages from God to us. Interestingly enough, they did this not only before the cross, but also after. Through the sacrifice of Jesus we are made God's children, and we have full access to the Father. Nevertheless, angels continue to come and bring messages to us, and they interact with us in ways that God could do directly Himself. Couldn't God have set Peter free from jail? Of course He could! Yet He chose to send an angel to do so. God still sends His angels today to interact with us. Watch out, because you never know when a heavenly postman will knock at your door.

Matthew 1:20; 2:13, 19–20; 28:5–7

Luke 1:11, 19, 26–38; 24:4–7

Acts 1:10–11; 8:26; 10:3–6, 22

Revelation 14:6–7

3. Angels are sent to bring healing.

There are not many passages that refer to angels bringing healing, but there are at least two. The passage from Matthew 8 does not mention angels specifically. I do believe, nonetheless, that they are at work in the story it tells. Their participation is implicit in the passage. The centurion implies that Jesus has servants under His command, and Jesus does not correct him. Rather, Jesus praises him for his faith, and the servant is healed immediately. No human could have run to the centurion's house fast enough and prayed for the servant's healing in time enough for that to happen. And the text says that the servant was healed the very *moment* Jesus said so. Only an angel could have been that fast. The angels are in the backdrop of this text. It is not openly stated, but clearly they are present. The passage from John 5 does specifically mention the presence of an angel, at least in the King James Version. Make sure you read it in that translation, because some other translations may not mention the angel.

Matthew 8:5–13

John 5:4 (KJV)

4. Angels are sent to reveal future events.

Angels come to bring us knowledge of future events. Most of the time this concerns God's plan for the future of His chosen ones as a whole, as a nation—not only the nation of Israel, but also including us, the Gentiles who were grafted into the olive tree as part of His holy nation (see Romans 11:17; 1 Peter 2:9). I cannot think of one account in the Bible where an angel brings an individual a revelation that does not affect Israel and the Church of our Lord Jesus Christ as a whole. Having said that, I do not doubt that God could do such a thing. I have not had that kind of experience with angels, yet I do long for it. I pray that in our devotional lives and in our search for more of God, we will be open to receiving a message from an angel concerning the future events in our personal lives.

Genesis 16:10–12

Judges 2:1–4; 13:3–7

2 Kings 1:3–4

Zechariah 2:3–12; 3:6–10; 4; 5.

Daniel 7:16; 8:15–19; 9:21–23; 10:14

Matthew 1:20–23

Luke 1:11–17, 26–38

5. *Angels are sent to give instructions.*

I hate to read instructions, mostly because most of the manuals that contain instructions are not at all user-friendly. They are a bunch of pages with lots of tiny little letters, and very few have any drawings or pictures in them. Instructions can be tough to read. But if an angel comes to bring us instructions, that is a totally different story. The manual would not be filled with boring black-and-white pages. Rather, it would be a glorious 3-D encounter that would forever change our lives, wouldn't it? I want to encourage you to ask the Father to send you angels who bring you instructions for your life.

Genesis 16:9; 19:1–22; 22:11–12; 31:11–13

Numbers 22:35

Judges 6:14, 20–21; 13:5, 13–14

1 Kings 19:5

2 Kings 1:3, 15

Zechariah 2:3–4; 3:3–5

Matthew 1:20; 2:13, 19–20

Acts 10:3–6; 12:8

6. *Angels are sent to bring encouragement.*

Who does not like receiving a word of encouragement, especially if it comes from a celestial being? I think that just seeing an angel, we would already be encouraged. How much more so if we receive an encouraging word from one!

Genesis 21:17–19

Daniel 10:12

Acts 27:23–24

7. Angels are sent to serve and strengthen.

This is one of my favorite angelic functions, to serve and strengthen us. Who would not like angels to serve and strengthen them? You know what? I think that many times, you and I have been served and strengthened by angels without even knowing it.

Daniel 10:8–11, 16–19

Matthew 4:11

Mark 1:13

Luke 22:43

8. Angels are sent to bring food.

Based on Psalm 78:25, some authors say that manna is the food of the angels, the food they eat up in heaven: "Human beings ate the bread of angels; he [the Lord] sent them all the food they could eat." Whether that is true or not, the fact remains that angels brought many people food in the Bible, including Jesus. How wonderful would it be to have an angel wearing a T-shirt that says *Papa Yahweh's Pizza* knocking at your door?

1 Kings 19:5–8

Psalm 78:25

Matthew 4:11

Mark 1:13

9. Angels are sent to protect and deliver.

I do believe that far more times than we are aware of, we have angels protecting and delivering us from harm. In the following Scriptures we have promises and accounts of God's angels watching over us, His children.

Genesis 19:1, 11, 15

Numbers 20:16

Psalm 34:7; 91:11–12

Isaiah 63:9

Daniel 3:17–28; 6:22

Matthew 26:53

Acts 5:17–20; 12:5–10

10. *Angels are sent to bring revelation.*

God sends His angels with revelation to us, His servants, so that we can cooperate with Him and accomplish His divine plan. It is an honor for us to be part of God's plan for mankind, and each one of us has a part to play.

Daniel 4:13, 17

Zechariah 1:9–19; 4:1–6, 11–14; 5:1–3

Acts 7:53

Galatians 3:19

Hebrews 2:2

Revelation 17:7–18; 22:6, 16

11. *Angels are sent to bring God's children up to heaven.*

God's angels are also our guides to our encounter with the Lord in heaven, not only for those of us who die, but also on that glorious day when we who remain will meet up with Him in the clouds.

Luke 16:22 (the people who die)

Matthew 24:31 (the living at the Second Coming)

12. *Angels are sent to execute God's judgment.*

I know that people don't like the idea of God sending His angels to do the "dirty work," but the Bible does show us that God sends His angels to execute His judgments. They come to take care of some uncomfortable situations, such as destroying Sodom and Gomorrah and killing thousands of enemy soldiers. I have talked to many people with questions about that, and the answer is simple: God created angels to minister to mankind, not to Himself. God is almighty and all-powerful. He does not need anyone to do anything for Him. He needs merely to wish or speak His will into existence, and it will be so. He uses angels to take care of the mess mankind makes, because, as I stated at the start, angels are humanity's nannies of a sort. Who do you think should clean up the messes babies make? That's right—the nannies. This is why God uses the angels to do some of the "dirty work." In part, it is why they were created. (Just to clarify, Matthew 24:31 is not a text about the angels executing judgment; rather, it is a verse about the angels gathering God's chosen people and delivering them from judgment.)

Genesis 19:1–25

2 Samuel 24:16–17

2 Kings 19:35

Psalm 35:5; 78:49

Isaiah 37:36

1 Chronicles 21:15

2 Chronicles 32:21

Ezekiel 9:1–7

Matthew 13:41–42, 49–50; 24:31

Acts 12:23

Revelation 7:1–2; 8:2–13; 9:15; 15:1

Watch for the Angels

God has assigned the angels to serve us and intervene in human history at His command. He has even assigned personal guardian angels to you and every other person on the planet. Now that you know more about the angels and all that they do, you can expect them to intervene in your life and you can watch for them. Be expectant and be watchful for the ministry of angels in your life.

Always keep in mind that God is a good Father who sends angels—your angels—to watch over you. Try to make a habit of including requests for angelic intervention when you pray to Him. The next time you pray, ask your Father to send His angels into your situation. When I pray, I have made it a habit to ask the Father to send His angels to help me in diverse situations. Ever since I have done that, my experiences with the angels have increased exponentially.

I want to encourage you to walk in an awareness of the presence and ministry of the angels over your life. I encourage you to pray to the Father often about sending them to help you and serve you, according to His sovereign will. Ask Him to open your eyes to see the angels, and even (why not?) to allow you to interact with angels and talk to them.

I want to pump some expectation into your heart. Pray and believe for God to send His angels to bring you messages in your dreams and even in person. When they do so, don't be afraid to ask them questions. Mary talked to an angel; Zechariah talked to an angel. Why not you?

The Christian life is not supposed to be a boring wait for death, so that we can go up to heaven. Jesus came so that we can live exciting supernatural lives filled with power, healing, supernatural manifestations and, of course, angels. Get ready in your spirit to have some powerful encounters with them! And remember, when you do see an angel, try to prevent your knees from knocking together, and tell the angel, "I know, I know, *fear not*, right?"

Notes

Chapter 1: Angelic Encounters

1. *Blue Letter Bible* Lexicon: Strong's G3008, s.v. "*leitourgeō*," https://www.blueletterbible.org/lang/lexicon/lexicon.cfm?strongs=G3008&t=KJV.

2. *Blue Letter Bible* Lexicon: Strong's 8064, s.v. "*shamayim*," https://www.blueletterbible.org/lang/lexicon/lexicon.cfm?t=kjv&strongs=h8064.

3. Other such passages are Ephesians 3:9–10 and Revelation 10:6.

4. *Blue Letter Bible* Lexicon: Strong's G32, s.v. "*aggelos*," https://www.blueletterbible.org/lang/lexicon/lexicon.cfm?t=kjv&strongs=g32.

5. *Blue Letter Bible* Lexicon: Strong's H4397, s.v. "*mal'ak*," https://www.blueletterbible.org/lang/lexicon/lexicon.cfm?t=kjv&strongs=h4397.

6. H. Wayne House and Timothy J. Demy, *Answers to Common Questions about Angels and Demons* (Grand Rapids, Mich.: Kregel, 2011), 13.

7. *Blue Letter Bible* "Search the Bible" feature, KJV and NIV versions, s.v. "angel" and "angels," https://www.blueletterbible.org.

Chapter 2: Healing in Their Wings

1. For a fuller explanation of why we should ask people's names when we pray for them, please refer to chapter 1 of my book *Be Healed and Stay Healed* (Chosen, 2016). Briefly, it has to do with being motivated by love.

2. You may notice a few places in which I refer to an angel as masculine, using *he* or *him*. I don't believe angels have a gender; they are spiritual beings without carnal flesh (see again Hebrews 1:14). Matthew 22:30 tells us that angels do not marry, implying that they are asexual: "At the resurrection people will neither marry nor be given in marriage; they will be like the angels in heaven." Yet our artwork often pictures angels as either male or female, and in my wording I am following the pattern of both the Greek and Hebrew languages, where the word *angel* is always masculine.

Chapter 3: "Pleez, Dun Shoo!"

1. Connie Cass, "AP-GfK Poll: Why do kids have faith in Santa? Because parents do; 8 in 10 grown-ups believed as tots," Associated Press, December 23, 2011, http://ap-gfkpoll.com/featured/ap-gfk-poll-december-2011-santa-topline.

Chapter 6: Guardian Angels

1. *Blue Letter Bible* Lexicon: Strong's G846, s.v. "*autos*," https://www.blueletter bible.org/lang/lexicon/lexicon.cfm?t=kjv&strongs=g846.

Chapter 7: They Come When We Worship

1. For more on the 10-step deliverance model, see Randy Clark's *Ministry Team Training Manual* (Global Awakening, 2012).

Chapter 9: They Come Bringing Gifts

1. In Christian theology, the tripartite view—trichotomy—holds that humans are a composite of three distinct components: *body, soul* and *spirit.* This contrasts with the bipartite view—dichotomy—where the *soul* and *spirit* are considered to be two different terms for the same part or entity. For more on this, see the *Wikipedia* article "Tripartite (theology)," https://en.wikipedia.org/wiki/Tripartite_(theology).

2. *Bible Study Tools: Scofield Reference Notes* (1917 ed.) online, "Matthew 27," http://www.biblestudytools.com/commentaries/scofield-reference-notes/matthew/matthew-27.html.

3. For more testimonies and teachings about healing, please refer to my book *Be Healed and Stay Healed* (Chosen, 2016).

Chapter 10: Seeing Angels

1. *BIBLETOOLS:* Topical Studies, "Bible Verses about Angels Eat Human Food," quote from John W. Ritenbaugh's "Image and Likeness of God" Part 3, http://www.bibletools.org/index.cfm/fuseaction/Topical.show/RTD/CGG/ID/13696/Angels-Eat-Human-Food.htm.

2. We do not know if the angels have the permanent ability to materialize or if that is something God does according to His divine purposes. Either way, the Bible shows us that angels do materialize and interact with people.

3. Surely Abraham did not bring the angels food to hold with their bare hands, as it would not have been considered clean. We can safely assume that Abraham brought them some sort of plate on which the food was placed. There are also other passages where angels touch objects, such as in the case of Gideon in Judges 6:21.

Chapter 11: Feathers

1. Kris Vallotton is a senior associate leader at Bethel Church and is also co-founder and overseer of Bethel School of Supernatural Ministry (BSSM).

2. Kris Vallotton (blog), "Raising the Dead, Gold Dust and Feathers," April 20, 2016, http://krisvallotton.com/raising-the-dead-gold-dust-and-feathers/.

3. *Wikipedia*, s.v. "Angels in art," last modified May 6, 2016, https://en.m.wiki pedia.org/wiki/Angels_in_art#In_Christian_art.

Chapter 12: Signs That Make You Wonder

1. Some of this information on tooth fillings was taken from Terry Donovan, DDS, R.J. Simonsen, DDS, MSy G. Guertin, DDS, MSEdz R.V. Tucker, DDS, "Masters of Esthetic Dentistry: Retrospective Clinical Evaluation of 1,314 Cast Gold Restorations in Service from 1 to 52 Years," *Journal of Esthetic and Restorative Dentistry* 16, no. 3 (2004): 194–203.

2. Khodadad E. Keith, *The Social Life of a Jew in the Time of Christ*, 5th ed. (London: Church Missions to the Jews, 1959), 55.

3. *Wikipedia*, s.v. "Dowry," last modified August 31, 2016, https://en.wikipedia.org/wiki/Dowry.

4. Jonathan Edwards, *The Works of Jonathan Edwards* (Carlisle, Penn.: Banner of Truth, 1991) 37–38.

Chapter 13: Angels in Your Life

1. For more information on this hierarchy model, see the *Wikipedia* article "Christian angelology," https://en.wikipedia.org/wiki/Christian_angelology.

Ed Rocha is senior leader and founder of the Pier49 Movement in Rio de Janeiro, Brazil, and is also an international speaker for Global Awakening Ministries. With over 25 years of ministry experience, Ed has preached in more than 20 countries, bringing a message of revival, healing and miracles wherever he goes. He has a Christian ministries degree from the International Bible Institute of London and a theology degree from PUC-Rio, and he currently is also pursuing master's degrees in both theology and teaching.

During his time in London, Ed received a strong impartation and experienced the Holy Spirit in a powerful way. This prophetic encounter prepared him to receive a direct impartation for healing ministry from Randy Clark, his spiritual mentor and father, in 2005. After this impartation, Ed began to see healings, signs and wonders flow in his life and ministry. Today, Ed ministers all over Brazil, North America and Europe. His revival meetings are marked by a strong presence of God, words of knowledge, healings and powerful impartations.

Ed and his wife, Dani, live in Rio de Janeiro, Brazil. For more information about Ed Rocha and his ministries, please visit any of the following websites: www.pier49.org, www.edrocha .org, www.h2ooficial.com or www.globalawakening.com/home /speakers/ed-rocha.

You can also find Ed on Facebook: www.facebook.com/edss rocha, www.facebook.com/H2Ooficial or www.facebook.com /pier49movement.

More from Ed Rocha

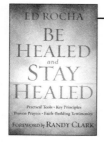

When Ed Rocha started in healing ministry, he encountered a sad reality: not everyone he prayed for was healed, and not everyone who gets healed stays healed. Why? Armed with faith in the finished work of Christ, Rocha sought biblical answers. Now he shares practical, spiritual tools to help you move in God's power and see more lasting results when you pray.

Be Healed and Stay Healed
edrocha.org

 **Chosen**

 Stay up to date on your favorite books and authors with our free e-newsletters. Sign up today at chosenbooks.com.

 Find us on Facebook. facebook.com/chosenbooks

 Follow us on Twitter. @Chosen_Books